BASICS

INTERACTIVE DESIGN

Gavin Allanwood
Peter Beare

USER EXPERIENCE DESIGN

CREATING DESIGNS USERS REALLY LOVE

Fairchild Books
An imprint of Bloomsbury Publishing Plc

50 Bedford Square	1385 Broadway
London	New York
WC1B 3DP	NY 10018
UK	USA

www.bloomsbury.com

Bloomsbury is a registered trade mark of Bloomsbury Publishing Plc

First published 2014

British Library Cataloguing-in-Publication Data
A catalogue record for this book is available from the British Library.

ISBN
PB: 978-2-940496-13-6
ePDF: 978-2-940447-69-5

Library of Congress Cataloging-in-Publication Data
Allanwood, Gavin.
User experience design : creating designs users really love / Gavin Allanwood and Peter Beare.
pages cm
Includes bibliographical references and index.
ISBN 978-2-940496-13-6 (alk. paper) -- ISBN 978-2-940447-69-5 (alk. paper)
1. Design--Human factors. 2. Design--Methodology. I. Beare, Peter, 1970- II. Title.
NK1520.A45 2013
745.4--dc23
2013020874

Printed and bound in China

0.0
Urban Screen
Gigantic fingers appear to distort the walls of the Kunsthalle building in Hamburg, via a projection from Urban Screen (see page 52).

It is reassuring to know that the physical book you are holding will not spontaneously reorganize, change content or disappear without trace. In the digital world such effects are common, and the idea of infinite space and variability takes a little getting used to. Modern devices offer countless ways for designers to deliver, update and manage content for users. These awesome new powers of communication need to be applied with user interaction in mind.

Here the architecture of this book is presented for your cognitive pleasure. Once the pattern is recognized and you have made a few visits to the pages within, you will understand the book's structure and recognize where it starts and where it ends. You may even work out the approximate position of a page that you want to revisit based on its visual character and relative position in this overview. And if you hadn't read this short explanation you would probably have done all that without thinking. Welcome to *User Experience Design*.

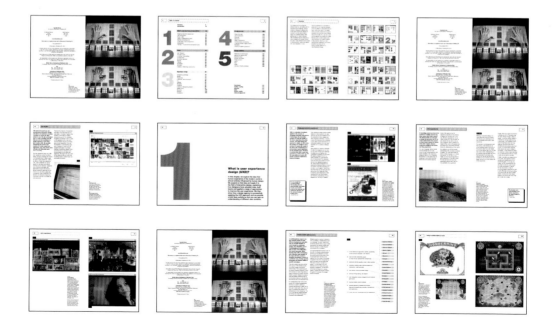

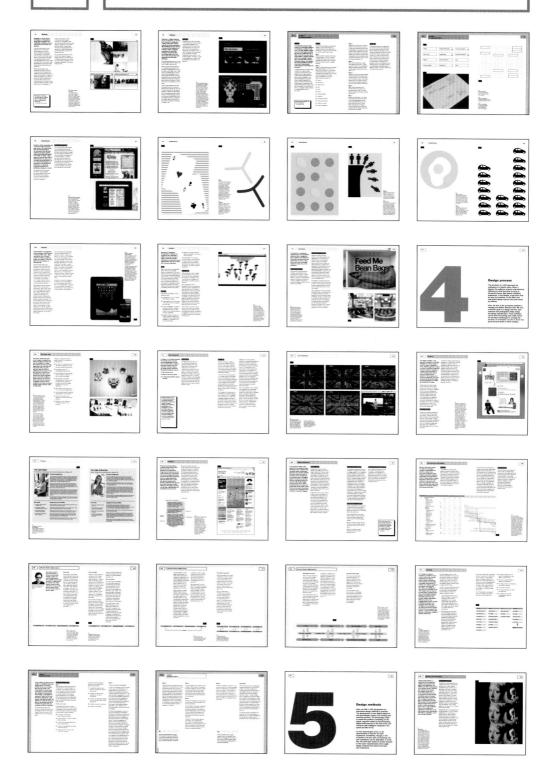

This book is for you if you are learning about interactive design and plan to be involved in creating a product or service for other people to use. We aim to introduce you to a way of thinking that will help you see that excellence in design depends on more than just creative skills. By carefully considering the factors that combine to create a good user experience, your work will be more effective and ultimately much more rewarding.

The user experience design tag 'UXD' when applied to creative interactive design conveys a message that means 'we understand what it takes to give our users a good experience'. UXD is an offshoot of plain user experience 'UX', a set of methods that can be applied to just about every activity involving human interaction. Designers who understand and apply UXD approaches can give their clients a strong competitive advantage. As we move into an era where a great deal of published media is expected to be dynamic and interactive it becomes much more important to consider the user experience.

There are five chapters, five practical exercises, three interviews and one case study in this book. Together they combine to demystify the subject and provide you with the necessary foundation knowledge to start to apply a UXD approach to your own work. The first chapter will get you thinking about human experience; then you will progress to understanding users, and in chapters 3, 4 and 5 you will recognize and apply the principal methods of experience design. At the end of the book we introduce tools and processes for evaluating user experience. We expect that your users will be delighted with your work and it is always good to record those nice comments somewhere.

0.1

0.2

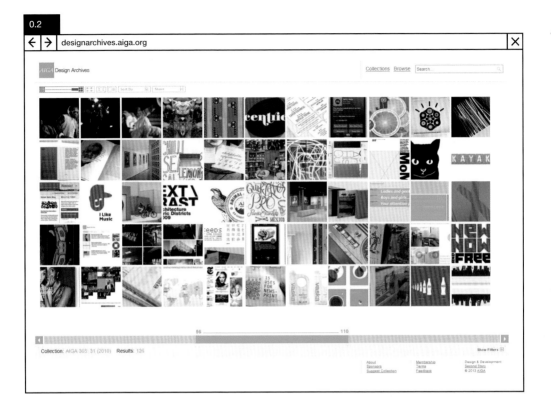

0.1
A UXD approach
At the time of writing there is strong demand for people who can apply a UXD approach, including skills in user research, responsive design and the optimization of website traffic.

0.2
AIGA Design Archives
created by Second Story
The design incorporates many tools for browsing and offers the user plenty of opportunity for research and discovery.

What is user experience design (UXD)?

In this chapter, we explore the idea that human experience of the modern world is almost entirely influenced by human design. We expand on that idea and apply it to the field of interactive design, explaining how designers have adopted roles, built teams and applied a range of approaches to improve the user experience. We then show how a design agency is successfully applying the UXD approach and we provide a brief team activity so that you can gain an understanding of different user contexts.

UXD is a collection of methods applied to the process of designing interactive experiences. It encourages the interactive designer to make the quality of the users' experience the prime concern. The logic behind this approach is simple. In UXD terms, the product of a design is only a success if it meets the needs of the client who commissioned it and provides a good experience for the intended users. Products or services that offer a poor user experience, or fail to keep up with the expectations of users, will sooner or later be replaced by improved designs.

User experience design needs a careful balance of what is good for the user and what can be accomplished within the constraints of time, budget and other resources. Generally, it requires a team effort because what is required to give users a good experience is not immediately apparent and may need expertise from a number of different areas.

More people are needed to advocate the idea that designers can do more for their users. People who challenge the status quo and highlight the unintelligent, frustrating and generally life-sapping designs that dim our world. Perhaps you could become one of these people? For inspiration there are some great people out there who are now regarded as gurus of UX. These include Donald Norman, described by *Business Week* as 'one of the world's most influential designers' and also 'a curmudgeon', Steve Krug who has written an internationally best-selling book *Don't Make Me Think: A Common Sense Approach to Web Usability* (2000) and Jakob Neilsen's who has been described by *Internet Magazine* as 'The King of Usability'.

'It's not enough that we build products that function, that are understandable and usable, we also need to build products that bring joy and excitement, pleasure and fun, and yes, beauty to people's lives.'
– Donald Norman

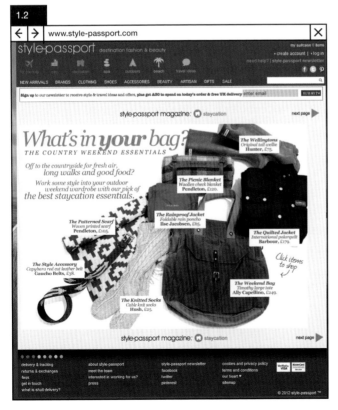

1.1–1.2
Style-Passport website
The website for Style-Passport (style-passport.com, designed by Maek) does more than emulate the visual design of glossy fashion magazines. The archetypal user will often make decisions about fashion and shopping that considers complex factors such as what-goes-with-what and who-else-is-wearing-it. The website has a structure and appearance that understands and facilitates this type of behaviour. UXD is about understanding the users and their context, rather than trying to impress them with visual flair.

If everything around you that is the product of a design process was taken away, what would remain? The climate defies our attempts to design its behaviour and so we create environments that protect us from it when needed. In almost every other respect, humans create the conditions that define our living experience.

Our use of language, fashion trends and the development of music evolve through human behaviour and social interaction. User experience designers need to try to understand the behaviour of the people they are designing for and create work that blends well with evolved systems.

Much of the quality of our life experience depends on the products of design that we encounter on our way. We have expectations, we can make choices and, if we are lucky, we can choose how we want to live our lives. Designers need to consider the impact of their work on the people they are designing for and create work that shows an understanding of their needs.

As a designer you will find yourself contributing to the universe of products of design. Your work may impact on small numbers of people, or on whole populations. You will want it to fit neatly into their lives and give them a good experience. If they don't notice the care and hard work you have expended to achieve this, then you have probably done a good job.

1.3

Context

Working in interactive design it is most likely that what you produce will become just a small part of all that contributes to the users' wider experience.

For example, the development team that builds a user interface for an airline booking website will focus on the airline's objective to sell tickets and fill their planes. But to do this they also need a wider understanding of why people travel and other elements that help build the complete user experience. We can say with some confidence that air travel is part of a bigger scenario and is not usually the whole experience.

A wider view encourages us to think of a holiday as a form of recreation that will mean different things to different people. It could be a family holiday or a holiday for a loving couple starting a relationship. It will probably involve travel and perhaps travel over long distances. We could draw links to diet because some people enjoy food tourism, or a link to health because some people may need a holiday to convalesce. In user experience design it is important to take a really wide view from the start because what you create is really just one part of the story.

It helps if you define key requirements of the wider user experience before identifying the requirements of the contributing parts. In the case of a holiday, one key requirement for the user may be to sit on a warm beach and make sandcastles. To deliver that key requirement, a host of contributing design elements will need to work effectively, including providing information to the user about typical weather conditions for their chosen location at the time of year when they plan to take their holiday.

1.3
Successful
collaborative design
This well-trodden coastal path fulfils the requirements of users to take a scenic route while avoiding obstacles and the cliff edge. In this case, the path does not precisely follow the cliff edge and so a balance has been achieved between the need to take in the sea view and the need to make reasonable progress. This is evidence of successful collaborative design providing a good experience without any apparent design process.

'The broader one's understanding of the human experience, the better design we will have.'
– Steve Jobs

1.4

interactive.nfb.ca/#/outmywindow/

1.4–1.6
Out My Window
Life provides plenty of opportunities for sharing, exploring, achieving and giving. When we design experiences, we are often enhancing the everyday and the familiar, rather than reinventing it. The National Film Board of Canada has created a series of experimental interactive films called *Out My Window* by Katerina Cizek, they are a collection of personal perspectives on city living. The documentary provides new ways to experience a film, by introducing a degree of exploration, non-linearity and 360-degree views.

However, the novel features do not undermine the concept at the heart the experience: the millennia-old practice of telling stories that connect with the values that all human's share.

1.5

interactive.nfb.ca/#/outmywindow/

interactive.nfb.ca/#/outmywindow/

1.6

In the preceding pages, we've described UXD as an approach to design that makes it possible to achieve the goal of giving users a good experience. Because it is an approach and not a well-defined procedure, it is more difficult for design teams to adopt UXD than other, more prescriptive methods.

For this reason, many design teams include a member who has a specific responsibility to ensure that UXD happens. They will be enthusiastic supporters of the mission to achieve excellent user experiences, and they will ensure that everyone in the team understands the approach and the reasons behind it. As part of their role they will monitor and evaluate the success of UXD and the costs involved, making sure that the UXD approach provides a good return on investment (RoI) as well as producing much better designs. To do this they will create an organizational framework, set ground rules, manage the scope of projects and referee meetings to ensure that uninformed opinion does not prevail. A successful UXD 'referee' will achieve harmony in a design team where designers conceive good user experiences and system builders understand what they are being asked to build.

In a large interactive design team there are job titles that explicitly define the UX role as independent from any responsibility for production. These include:

➜ UXD Director

➜ Strategist

➜ User Evangelist

➜ Analyst

In many projects, UXD is a responsibility added to a development and production role such as:

➜ UX Designer

➜ UI Designer or Front-end Developer

➜ Software Engineer.

Employers often say they are looking for a 'team player' and by this they usually mean someone who will cooperate and communicate with the rest of the team. If your work is shrouded in mystery and you prefer to deliver a brainchild after weeks of solitary work in a hidden corner of the studio, then you will need to change your approach in order to be successful in UXD.

Michael J Godfrey
User Experience Design Director

Michael leads strategic development and user experience design for the studio. Working with content producers and visual designers, he guides the studio's approach to story structures, information architecture, physical experiences, interfaces and master plans.

Part of his job is to review all the teams' user experience approaches and maintain a high standard of excellence, and inspire the team to evolve the medium. Since experience design is a cross-disciplinary practice, the UX Design Director collaborates with and mentors fellow team members to develop visitor experiences that are engaging, intuitive and heartfelt. He works with the team to hone their skills in communicating their designs through the creation of compelling presentations, prototypes, proofs-of-concepts, mock-ups and video demos. Michael's role is to be a visionary and to adapt and defend that vision throughout the life of a project to both the internal and the client teams.

Jennifer Dolan
Content Producer

As a Content Producer at Second Story, Jen is involved throughout each project to help ensure the best union between content and user experience. Along with user experience designers and producers, she meets with clients at the beginning of projects to understand the content, audience, and desired experience for the project. As the project progresses, Jen works with the client to research, create and track content, and works with the internal team to ensure that designers have the materials they need to inform and support their work. During the early phases of a project, Jen is an advocate for the content with user experience and visual designers. In later phases, she keeps the end user at the forefront of her role of usability and functional tester, working with developers to bring the team's designs to life.

Norman Lau
User Experience Designer

The day-to-day work of a User Experience Designer at Second Story will cut across multiple projects and involve studio members from all disciplines. In the early stages of projects, Norman will participate in conversations with clients, producers, and content strategists to understand the context of the proposed design and to determine what audiences they are designing for. As a project proceeds, he will make design artefacts such as stakeholder maps, wireframes, and storyboards to help visual designers and developers understand the designed experience. Ultimately, a User Experience Designer needs to be able to work fluidly and to facilitate conversations between diverse perspectives in order to arrive at a design that is useful, usable, and desirable.

A multidisciplinary team is one that contains people of quite different backgrounds and skills who are brought together to work closely on a particular project. The 'discipline' part of 'multidisciplinary' provides a clue to some of the difficulties that teams encounter. When learning their skill or developing their expertise each member of the team will have needed to discipline themselves to focus on a particular area, develop specific knowledge and become skilled in specific techniques.

They will probably have done all this with a group of like-minded people who share a range of social and cultural ideas. This is good because we expect a systems engineer to work with precision to make things that are highly functional and efficient. We also expect a graphic designer to produce work that applies visual language to communicate ideas and meaning that can influence us on an emotional level.

A multidisciplinary team will contain people with a range of perspectives and this can result in additional creativity and synergy of ideas. As the team get to know each other, they will begin to recognize and consider the perspectives of other disciplines. This in turn will help the creative process, generating new ideas through team interaction and collaboration.

Bringing together a group of people to form an effective multidisciplinary team is a challenge. The team needs to be sufficiently diverse with a range of skills balanced for the relevant project and dynamic enough to enable frequent and effective communication.

It is a good approach to build a team at the start of a project so that the team structure can be planned to achieve the specific goals of the project. Even if a particular team member is not required from the outset of the project, it is good to have them recognized as part of the team from the beginning. If the team is built at the start of a project, it is more likely to be fully informed and committed all the way through to completion. The structure of the team will depend on various factors, including the people available, the goals of the project, the budget and the timescale.

1.7
Features of a design and development team
The standard ISO 9241-210 (see page 131) lists ten skill areas for a human-centred design and development team. This chart attempts to match some of the more common skills with a corresponding main skill area from the ISO 9241-210 list. When building a team it is important to decide what each member's job title is, because these are labels that allow others to instantly relate what they do to what *they think* you do. The process of working towards a common goal of creating an excellent user experience can help a multidisciplinary team to work together.

1.7

1) human factors and ergonomics, usability, accessibility, human-computer interaction, user research;

2) users and other stakeholder groups (or those that can represent their perspectives);

3) application domain expertise, subject matter expertise;

4) marketing, branding, sales, technical support and maintenance, health and safety;

5) user interface, visual and product design;

6) technical writing, training, user support;

7) user management, service management and corporate governance;

8) business analysis, systems analysis;

9) systems engineering, hardware and software engineering, programming, production/manufacturing and maintenance;

10) human resources, sustainability and other stakeholders

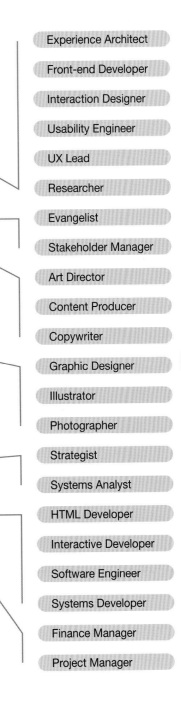

Experience Architect

Front-end Developer

Interaction Designer

Usability Engineer

UX Lead

Researcher

Evangelist

Stakeholder Manager

Art Director

Content Producer

Copywriter

Graphic Designer

Illustrator

Photographer

Strategist

Systems Analyst

HTML Developer

Interactive Developer

Software Engineer

Systems Developer

Finance Manager

Project Manager

1.8

1.8
'Wondermind'

'Wondermind' is a collection of online games and interactive films designed to teach the principles of neuroscience to children. The uniting theme of the site is 'Alice in Wonderland', and it coincided with a Tate Liverpool exhibition about the works of Lewis Carroll.

The site is designed by Preloaded, a multidisciplinary team with skills in development, design, user experience and entrepreneurship. The award-nominated games are the result of collaboration between Preloaded and educators, physiologists, scientists, gallery curators, film-makers and others.

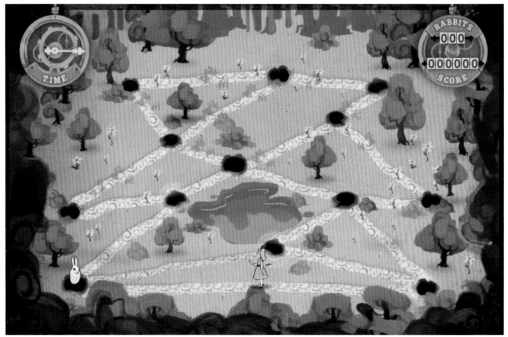

Over 100 years ago, Henry Ford is reported to have said that if he asked customers what they wanted they would have replied 'faster horses'. This quotation is sometimes used by those who question the idea of centring the design process on the user. When leaps in technology come along, such as the invention of the motor car and the production line, a 'user' is not in a position to conceive the potential impact on their experience. It is argued that users are inherently conservative and will often prefer a familiar design to a new and improved one.

History is peppered with attempts to formalize ways to find out what users want and to create a formula that guarantees success. UXD is fundamentally a UCD (User Centred Design) approach that also considers the user experience in the context of use.

Instead of asking what users want, we observe what their experience is and think of ways to improve it by using knowledge and skill. So in the Henry Ford example, we would recognize that faster and more flexible transportation was technically possible and we would work with users to see how this could improve their experience in the context of their daily lives.

Alternative approaches to UXD range from 'evolutionary design', in which case we really would be trying to breed faster horses, to 'expert review' where knowledgeable people decide what is best for us all.

1.9

'Task modelling' is a method used to analyse the tasks that a user needs to complete in order to reach a goal. Although good within a UXD approach, on its own it fails to fully consider the user experience or different contexts of use.

'Agile' software development, as the name suggests, is a method that promotes a fast and flexible approach to software development. Key features of the agile approach include team adaptability to changes in design direction and a willingness by developers to deliver, review and improve designs continually in an iterative cycle. Agile methods fit well within a UXD approach.

'Usability' is a method used to assess the quality of an interactive design. There are five components of a usability test: Learnability, efficiency, memorability, errors and satisfaction. Usability testing is a useful tool that can be used to discover what needs improving in an interactive design, either when complete or preferably during the development process.

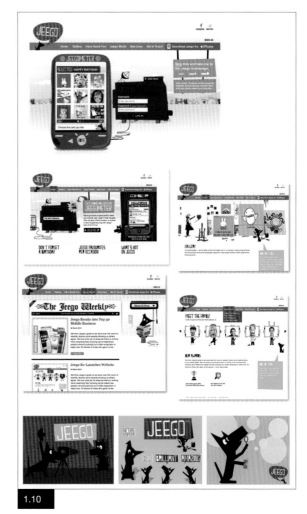

1.10

1.9–1.10
Jeego
Jeego is a service that allows users to send electronic greetings cards using their mobile phones, as well as a cheeky dog character that brings the brand to life.
The website and apps are designed around a number of principles: Is it easy to understand? Is it easy to use? Does it make me feel good? Behind each of these principles is a legacy of methods that have, over the years, been applied to improving the users' experience.

The project

The agency was asked to design and build a new website for The Car People, a regional Car Supermarket based in North West England with an annual turnover of £150m ($235m USD). A collaborative, multidisciplinary team was brought together featuring talent from many disciplines: including an account director, project manager, producer, creative developer, front-end developer and user experience architect.

The client

Code Computerlove actively invite the client to be part of the development team and give them the final say when it comes to prioritizing tasks. Clients take part in weekly iterative project reviews. Outside of these events, regular client communication is augmented using Redmine (an online, collaborative project management tool) which facilitates real-time sharing of information. This open approach is cited as a key element in Code's success in regularly building constructive relationships between teams and their clients. Openness and good quality feedback is considered to be one of the most important ingredients to building constructive relationships with clients (for more about clients as stakeholders see page 34).

User requirements

The team made sure that they knew everything about the car buyer and what they require from a car website by putting together competitive reviews, hosting focus groups, interviews and studying website analytics. This information allowed them to develop a deep understanding of their users' needs.

User journeys

User journeys helped the team to conceptualize and structure the website's content and functionality. User journey's force a shift away from thinking about structure in terms of hierarchies or a technical build. It requires the team to consider the logical paths a user would take through their online journey: how they would find the website, navigate to relevant content, and then arrive at a point of conversion such as a purchase or request for more information. This approach helps to create focus within the design team, ensuring that decisions are based on fact rather than assumption.

Established in
1999

Based in
Manchester, UK

— 70 employees
— Independently owned (and massively proud of it).
— A mix of strategy, user experience, search and media, creative and technical expertise.
— The most awarded UK agency outside of London.
— Design teams manage a stimulating design space where walls are covered with project information: including user research, wireframes, visual designs, questions, ideas, and project and task status.

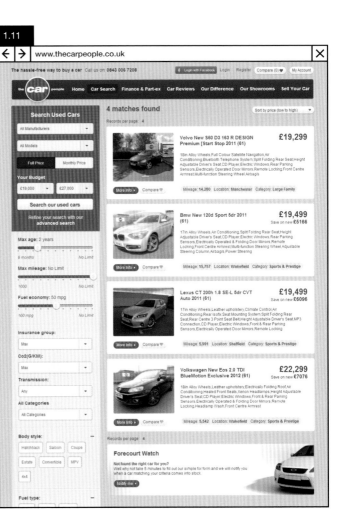

1.11
Optimizing the site
Since the initial go live, Code have been continually optimizing the The Car People site. This has been informed by user feedback, further user testing, site analytics, expert reviews and A-B testing.

Design

A PET toolkit (persuasion, emotion and trust) was used alongside classic usability techniques to add a layer of psychology and human understanding to improve the effectiveness of the design. 'Card Sorting' and 'Tree Testing' techniques involved end users in the website structuring process and helped to validate the thinking of the team.

Wireframes and simple prototypes allowed the team to test ideas quickly and evaluate client and user responses to aspects of the visual design and functionality of the product.

User testing

An in-house facility was used to observe and record mouse actions and comments made by 'real' users performing tasks in a script devised by the development team.

Optimization

Since the launch day the team have continually optimized the site in response to user feedback, further user testing, site analytics, expert reviews and A-B testing.

1.12
Code Computerlove
Code Computerlove took a user-centred approach to designing The Car People web-site, putting their client's customers at the heart of the process.

1.12

1.13

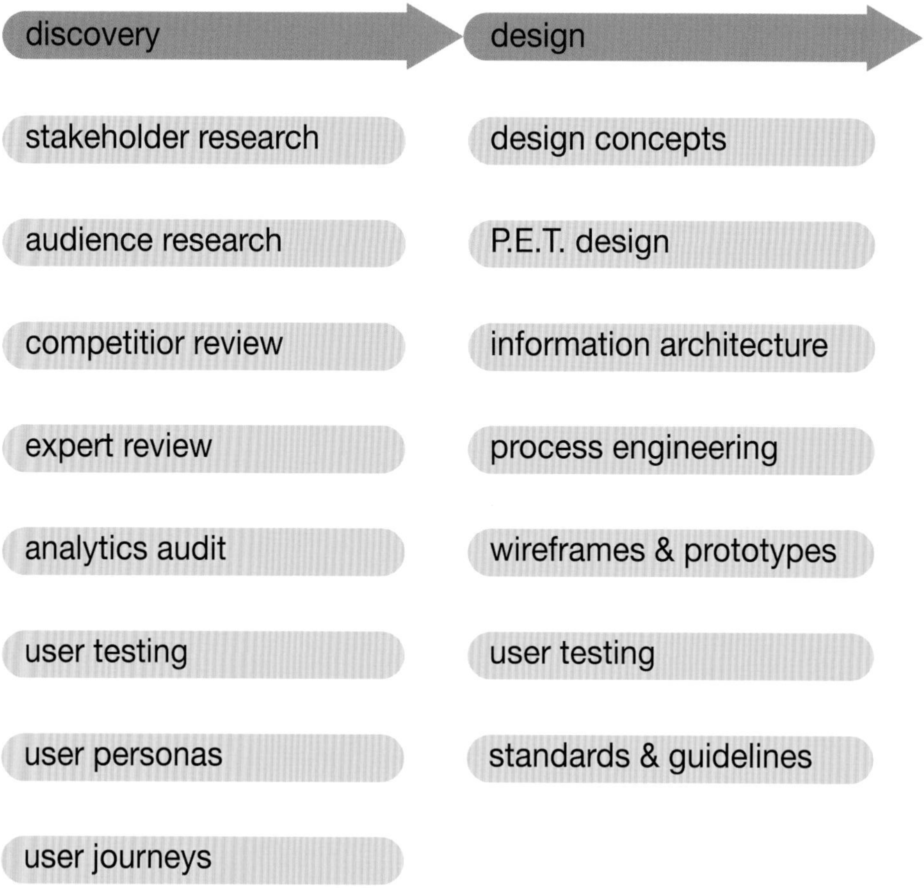

discovery ➜ | design ➜

discovery

- stakeholder research
- audience research
- competitior review
- expert review
- analytics audit
- user testing
- user personas
- user journeys

design

- design concepts
- P.E.T. design
- information architecture
- process engineering
- wireframes & prototypes
- user testing
- standards & guidelines

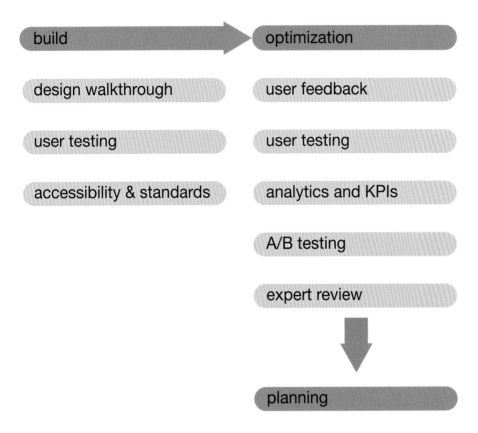

1.13
Identification of deliverables
To achieve success, a typical
project at Code will identify
many deliverables, going
through the stages of discovery,
design, build and optimization.

In every project there are stakeholders. It is obvious that the client has a big stake, and so do their employees and their customers. The design team has a stake because a successful project should pay the bills and salaries, provide job satisfaction and win awards. These are all key stakeholders, but there are likely to be others who should also be considered if the project is to be a success.

Stakeholders who will be affected by a project are said to have an interest in a project. Conversely, stakeholders who can affect a project are said to have power over a project. It is bad news when a stakeholder is not identified until it is too late. It means that the project has not considered their interest or power, and that may cause the project to fail in some way or, worse still, break a regulation or the law.

As part of the project management process a UXD team will need to:

➜ Identify all the stakeholders

➜ Rank them according to their importance to the success of the project

➜ Develop strategies for understanding their requirements

➜ Communicate with them and gain their involvement if necessary

➜ Manage their expectations and keep them happy.

One way to identify and rank stakeholders is to bring the team together with key stakeholders and build an influence/interest grid. Team members fill the grid with sticky notes naming all the stakeholder groups they can identify. Red notes are used for uninterested or unsupportive stakeholders, and green for those who are supportive. Each note is then placed on the grid in a position relative to the influence and interest of the named stakeholder. This technique helps to visualize the stakeholder 'body' and serves as a reminder to keep the most influential and interested involved in developments.

1.14

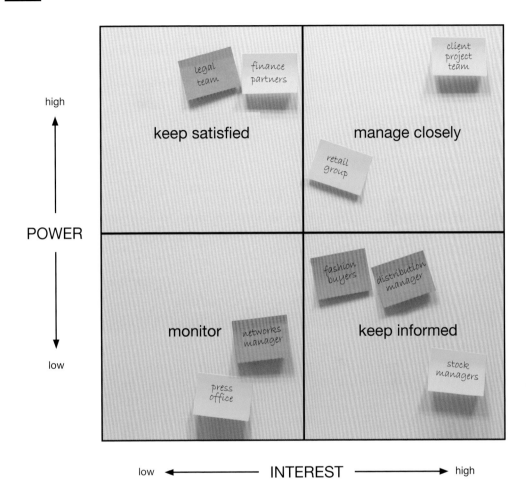

1.14
Influence grid
An influence/interest grid
representing stakeholders in a
project to deliver an online store
for a fashion retailer. Easy to
update, this simple device can
help to keep the project team
mindful of the impact of their
project in a wider context.

It is natural for designers to resist the constraints imposed on their creativity when designing for others. Even when the needs of users are carefully considered, the designer must also take account of the context in which the design will be used. This activity introduces the idea of an iterative process of design that focuses on a specific user group and context. It is best run with small teams of three to four. Each team will need some sticky notes, a timekeeper and someone nominated to write things down.

Follow each step in sequence and resist the temptation to read ahead if you can. The topic of this exercise is a food menu. Remember, it is the process that we are interested in rather than the topic!

Activity

Step 1 – quick solution
[Time allowed: ten minutes]

Work as a group to create a single three-course menu that every member of the team agrees would provide them with a great dining experience. Write each course on a separate sticky note and put all three in sequence on a suitable surface.

1.15

Step 2 – the user
[Time allowed: ten minutes]

Having arrived at a suitable menu as a team, you now need to consider if it is suitable for a specific user group. Write each user group listed below on a piece of paper and select one at random.

➜ six-year-old boys

➜ vegetarians

➜ honeymoon couples

➜ fashion models

Discuss the characteristics of the *user group* and make changes to any of the courses in the existing menu if doing so would provide a better user experience for them. Don't discard the original sticky note, just place any design revisions above it. Aim to make as few changes as possible.

Step 3 – the context
[Time allowed: ten minutes]

Now you have a suitable menu for your users, you need to consider the context in which it will be prepared and consumed. Write each context listed below on a piece of paper and select one at random from a hat or similar.

➜ a street cafe at 1pm on Sunday

➜ on holiday in a tent pitched in a field in Ireland with six other people

➜ a business class seat on an aircraft flying to Paris

➜ a hospital bed in a war zone

Discuss how the characteristics of the *context* will affect the user. Make changes to any of the courses in the existing menu if doing so would provide a better user experience for the user in the specific context. Again, keep the previous sticky note and place any design revisions above it. Aim to make as few changes as possible.

1.15
User and context
These four images, loaded with commonly understood cultural and contextual associations, remind us of the need to know more about our users and to consider their context.

Step 4 – analysis and review

[Time allowed: as long as you like]

You may have found that getting everyone in your team to agree on a single menu was difficult and perhaps compromises were needed to reach agreement? If this exercise was run before lunch then perhaps the 'great dining experience' may have been translated to 'something to satisfy my immediate hunger'.

How did your team relate to the user group chosen at random? Were generalizations and stereotypes evident, e.g. all small boys like chips or all fashion models eat green salad? Is this sensible and, if not, then how do designers 'connect' with their users?

Did the context make a difference? Should the context be considered earlier in the process? How can a user experience designer control the context in which their work is received?

Does the final menu still meet the requirements of Step 1? Have the changes that were made for the defined user and context made the menu unsuitable for all other users?

Outcomes

If the activity has been successful, you should by now begin to understand that the user and context are very important in creating a good user experience. You may have also found that introducing constraints to the design can actually be beneficial in clarifying the scope and providing a sharper focus for the design team. You may be surprised to find that the resulting design may be better at providing a good experience for more of the user groups than the initial design created at Step 1. You could test this by considering the final design against the other user groups and contexts listed.

1.16
Avoiding stereotypes
UX designers think sensitively about who the user may be and consider their context. Activity 1 reveals how an approach that uses general or stereotypical models of users can result in designs that fail.

1.16

Users

In this chapter, we explain how information about users can help you create designs that deliver a better experience. This is easier said than done because it is often unclear who will use a design, where they will use it and why they will use it. There is much less certainty about the user's motivations, expectations and experience when encountering a new interactive design.

The user's world is dynamic and complex and to understand it requires knowledge of user behaviour and the strategic use of research and development methods that are most likely to result in satisfying their expectations.

A UXD approach requires that the potential users of a new interactive design are considered early in the development of a project, throughout the project, prior to delivery and continually once the project is in active service. The rewards are tangible, including better performing designs and happier users.

Of course, it is possible to undertake projects without any user research. In such cases, the design will probably be shaped by the design team and their desire to satisfy the client. The resulting user experience may be good but is more likely to be poor or broken. As companies look to interactive media across the Web and mobile platforms to engage their customers, the consequences of ignoring users in a design and development process can be dire.

Because user research is best started at the beginning of a project, it may be too late to do user research halfway through. This is because by that time any changes may be too fundamental and too costly to implement. Projects can get trapped in a run of cumulative design decisions that make the end product less effective from the user's point of view. Good user research informs the design process in much the same way as making good technical decisions requires a good understanding of the technologies involved.

A list of requirements developed through good user research is a sensible starting point when considering the scope and functionality of a new system – although it will not in itself produce a plan for designers to follow. More work will be needed to interpret research results; and other factors, such as the availability of new technologies, will influence final design decisions.

Two basic questions to ask at the beginning of a new interactive design project are:

(1) Who will use it?

(2) What will it do?

Answering question 1 requires the use of demographic descriptors such as those in the following list.

At this early stage, it is necessary to narrow the field to 'primary users'. Doing so will not exclude other users (unless that is required) but it will provide a much better focus for the development team.

➜ Age range

➜ Ethnicity

➜ Experience

➜ Gender

➜ Income level

➜ Language

➜ Level of educational attainment

➜ Location

➜ Occupation or profession

➜ Religion

When responding to question 2 it is useful to think about the user's main aim in using the system that you are creating. Listing what the system needs in order for the user to achieve the aim is a good way to answer this question. The example shown below lists the requirements for a simple online transaction.

User aim: To purchase a new camera that takes good pictures and doesn't cost too much.

System requirements: the user should be able to:

➜ Select a product

➜ Make a purchase

➜ Arrange delivery

➜ Return a product

The next stage is to recruit a group of potential users who fit the demographic description defined in the answer to question 1. We can ask the group questions and subject them to a range of user research methods to find out what the system needs in order to provide them with a good user experience. This information will help the design team to produce a requirements statement that will provide essential guidance in the development of the project.

After a little user research, the initial requirements list can be expanded to include much more detail. A snippet to give you some idea of how this would progress is shown below.

System requirements:
the user should be able to:

➜ Select a product

➜ Search by type

➜ Read reviews

➜ Choose a colour

➜ Choose a size

➜ Select a quantity

and so on...

2.1

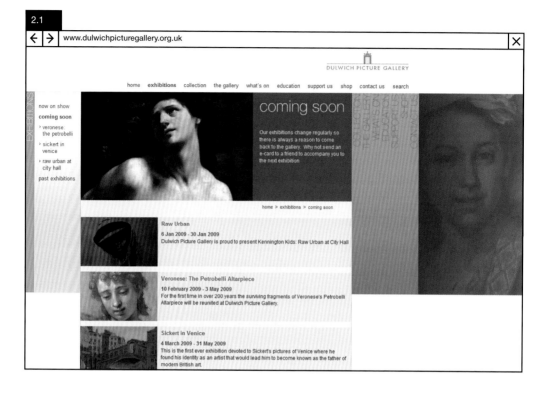

2.1
Dulwich Picture Gallery

Websites like the Dulwich Picture Gallery, with its unified colour scheme and subtle animations, may seem like an outcome of intuitive design. In truth, intuitive designs are the result of careful consideration and research into who the user is, and how they go about performing common tasks, such as scheduling a visit to an exhibition.

As well as a conventional navigation bar across the top of the site, visitors may 'glide' through the pages as if they were flicking through a print brochure. The site uses imperative language ('*plan your visit*', '*subscribe*', '*connect*'), as well as context-specific features such as maps and calendars. The site is a functional invitation to act and engage, rather than an inert fact sheet.

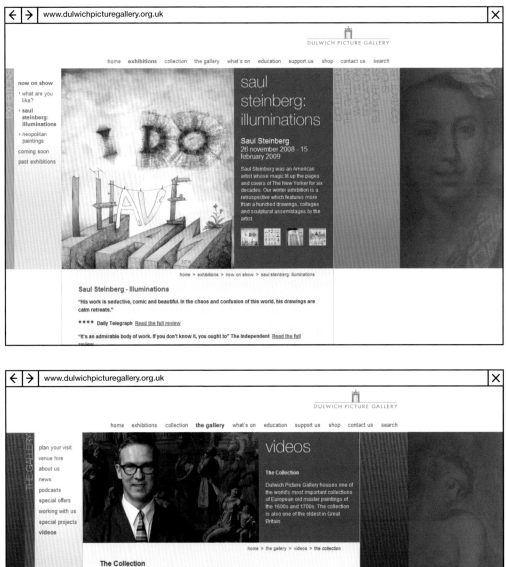

No project can take place without learning about the intended user and their context. There are a number of ways to find out about the user's world.

Surveys

Websites such as surveymonkey.com mean that it is easy to gather and collate quantitative and qualitative data. Response rates for surveys can be very low, but can be improved if the survey is kept short, with few open-ended questions, and if users are reminded to complete the survey via multiple channels.

Interviews and focus groups

One-to-one interviews help you to understand a sample of individuals in more detail. Focus groups are similar, but will typically involve six-to-ten users at once. The advantage here is that the dynamics within the group may bring up topics for discussion that would not arise in an interview situation.

Interviews, surveys and focus groups can be unreliable, as the participants may not be able to express their ideas accurately. Studying users in the field, although time-consuming and costly, may provide more faithful information.

Field studies

The purpose of observing users in the 'field' (the term 'ethnography' is sometimes borrowed from social sciences to describe this idea) is to challenge any assumptions that the designer may already have about the user group and their context. Field studies can provide abundant data, so it is a good idea to record as much as possible (ideally with video) so that user behaviour can be carefully examined later on.

Generative approaches

A more creative method is to ask users to generate research material, such as diaries. These can be written or audio/visual diaries, and allow users to document their daily activity. Designers can use these artefacts to probe feelings about relevant experiences. For other projects, users may model their own prototypes out of paper, clay, or construction toys.

2.2
Sqoshi

As more people engage in curating their own lives online, many social media websites can provide researchers with rich opportunities to find out about the lives of users. Sqoshi.com is a Keep It Usable project that encourages members to post images and stories about their favourite consumer products.

Lisa Duddington
Lisa is a usability, research and persuasive design specialist with over 12 years' experience.

Ricardo Ortega
Ricardo is an expert in mobile and web UX with over 14 years' experience of designing innovative interfaces and interactions for award-winning products.

Keep It Usable is an award-winning research and creative design agency, who specialize in usability testing and user experience design. They design interfaces for different platforms and research them with real users to be engaging, smart, simple, beautiful and profitable. Here, Lisa Duddington and Ricardo Ortega from Keep It Usable tell us about the way they understand the end users, in order to create a positive, profitable experience for products and services.

Is 'user experience design' a new approach?

The term 'user experience' is just the latest term of many used to describe how a person interacts with a digital or physical product or service. It is the most popular term so far and has definitely helped to describe what we do.

Where do you begin in working out who the 'user' is?

In most cases, the client will already understand who their target audience is and already be marketing towards a certain type of person, so a lot of this information already exists within a company. Our role is to find this information and translate it into personas (see page 114). To help with this we hold workshops with internal stakeholders to try to step into the users' shoes and understand who they are, and what they like and dislike. We gather data from numerous departments and may talk to representative customers to understand more about them. Personas are brilliant for many reasons. They enable us as an agency to understand who the target audience for a project is, so we can better meet their wants and needs via the design. It also means that we can visualize the correct target audience when we conduct user research so that the results reflect the wider audience.

Personas are great for the client, as it gives them a company-wide understanding of who their audience is. Personas enable everyone to see the user in the same light, which can prevent disagreement and misunderstanding between stakeholders, and also enables better decision making.

How do you find out about the user experience?

Our preferred method is ethnographic-style research (see the first column of 150). Observing and interviewing users in their environment in an everyday context shows a more natural interaction with the product or service being tested, and gives a truer reflection of the user experience.

We use lab-based usability testing techniques when stakeholders want to be more highly involved. If we are researching something that has already been tested previously, we will likely recommend eye tracking. Eye tracking technology enables us literally to see through the users' eyes; we can see where they are looking and for how long. This shows us what is capturing the users' attention and whether it is for the right or wrong reasons. We then redesign the interfaces to change the users' behaviour.

'Personas enable everyone to see the user in the same light, which can prevent disagreement and misunderstanding between stakeholders, and also enables better decision making.'

How useful do you find focus groups?

Focus groups are great for brainstorming ideas and generating discussion, but they are often mistaken for being a good user experience research tool. The difficulty is that people are highly influenced by other people. People with different personality types respond differently in group situations. Some will become incredibly opinionated; some will sit back and not say much at all; others will want to agree with the dominant person in the group. The results are not often a true reflection of each individual's honest opinion.

We prefer to recruit people ourselves to guarantee they correctly fit our target demographics. You need to create a set of questions to filter users into your target group. To find your users, think of where they hang out in real life or online and advertise there. For example, if you need students then put up posters around colleges and universities or on an online student forum.

Beyond the initial user research, are users involved at later stages of the process?

Of course. The ideal process is iterative, meaning that users are involved at every stage of the design process and there is a constant cycle of research and design. Early designs should be tested with rapid prototyping tools, which can then be quickly tested with users. You can even test rough sketches; they don't have to be finalized wireframes. The benefit of doing so is that nothing has been hard-coded at this stage so changes are easy, quick and much cheaper to implement.

Can you think of some of the instances where user profiling has really surprised you?

With experience, you begin to more easily and accurately foresee the problems people will encounter. However, user research is still often very surprising, which is why it is one of our favourite parts of analysing the user experience.

2.3
The User Experience Machine
In this poster designed by Keep It Usable, Lisa and Ricardo use a simple infographic to communicate the benefits of a UXD approach to their clients.

the user experience machine

keepitusable

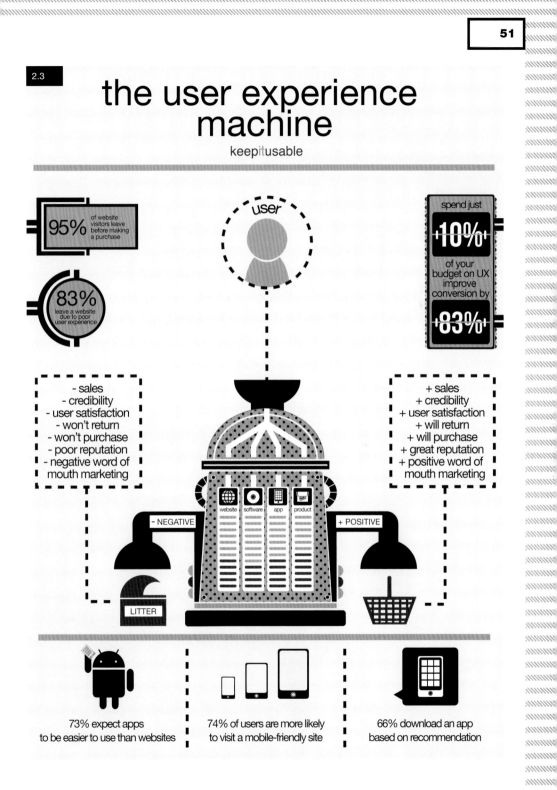

95% of website visitors leave before making a purchase

83% leave a website due to poor user experience

user

spend just 10% of your budget on UX improve conversion by 83%

- sales
- credibility
- user satisfaction
- won't return
- won't purchase
- poor reputation
- negative word of mouth marketing

+ sales
+ credibility
+ user satisfaction
+ will return
+ will purchase
+ great reputation
+ positive word of mouth marketing

website software app product

– NEGATIVE   + POSITIVE

LITTER

73% expect apps to be easier to use than websites

74% of users are more likely to visit a mobile-friendly site

66% download an app based on recommendation

Because we are social creatures, many of our experiences involve other people. Networked games and social websites clearly have a social purpose, but virtually all other experiences have a shared dimension: printing holiday snaps; booking a hotel; renewing your travel insurance; watching a video; ordering a meal; all of these may involve interaction with friends, colleagues, family-members, experts, or strangers.

The way we act with our families is different to the way we act with our friends. The way that we act with authority figures, such as a teacher, boss or doctor, is not the same way we act in the company of strangers. The important thing to recognize is that it is all an *act*: in different social situations, we perform a social role that is appropriate to the setting, and the people around us are an audience.

Typically, we show mutual respect for each other's social roles by using strategies such as cooperation, politeness, praise and deference. Rewarding co-experiences are ones that provide channels for this exchange of goodwill.

Even when experiences are solitary, they are the currency of social interaction. We talk about things we have done; things we have enjoyed; even negative experiences can yield amusing anecdotes.

When we talk about 'user context', we should consider more than the ergonomics of the spatial environment. We must also think about the social dimension of an experience, intended or not, and consider how that will affect our emotional response to the experience.

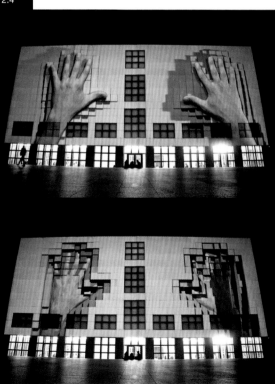

2.4

2.4
Urbanscreens
Moving images interplay with surfaces of buildings in a projection. Events like this are designed to be experienced by groups and individuals in public settings, but all experiences – even solitary ones – have the potential to live on in social media settings as users discuss, share and tweet their experiences.

Experiences can feel good, or they can feel bad. It is difficult to predict exactly what emotions an experience might provoke. But it is possible to understand some of the factors that influence our emotional responses, and the way that these can enhance or undermine an experience.

In his book *Emotional Design* (2005), Donald Norman categorizes three types of responses to designed products or experiences. He calls these responses: visceral, behavioural, and reflective.

Visceral, behavioural and reflective responses

Our initial 'gut' reaction is our visceral response; one which involves base instincts, such as fear, desire, attraction, repulsion, or shock. For example, the thrill of riding a rollercoaster is a typically visceral experience. Similarly, a sleek, weighty, smartphone may induce a visceral reaction just by holding it and gazing at its contours.

Behavioural responses consider function: how fully or easily something does the thing it is designed to do. Negative behavioural responses arise if an experience is frustrating or confusing. Positive behavioural responses arise from good ergonomics and good interaction design.

The function of a movie is to tell a story, which requires strong characters and an intriguing plot. This is why a 90-minute compilation of chase sequences would not produce a positive behavioural response in the audience, even though the spectacle may produce a viscerally satisfying hour-and-a-half.

A reflective response is one that activates our critical faculties. We evaluate and judge experiences against personal values, such as pride, cynicism, loyalty and self-image. Our enduring memories of an experience arise from reflections like this, and these may influence our future use of products or services.

At a reflective level, we may admire the elegance or cleverness of a design solution. We may be equally conscious of how others may perceive us as consumers or participants. Peer pressure may influence a user's reflective judgment, regardless of behavioural considerations such as usability or affordability, so it is worth observing the social dimension of user experience in your target users, and in the development of your designs.

2.5
The Spotify Box
For designer Jordi Parra, the idea of 'music as a gift' was an important emotional element of the concept behind the Spotify Box. The tokens represent different music play-lists; the proximity of the tokens alerts the box to play the appropriate tracks via the music-sharing platform. The discs provide a tactile, visceral pleasure to the experience of digital music, as well as the reflective, social experience of collecting and sharing.

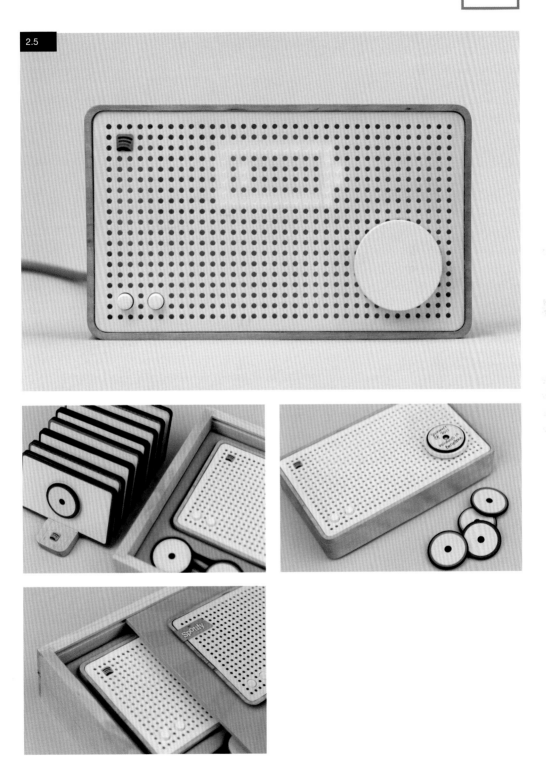

Experiences are often sequential, and occupy time, so the participant may have to retain key information from step to step. However, the capacity of people to remember things is limited. Designers can ease the mental load on the user by creating experiences that require understanding and recognition rather than recollection.

Short-term versus long-term memory

Our short-term memory is little more than a mental jotter: a temporary buffer for holding pertinent information. It is volatile, and only by a process of mental encoding can this information be stored more permanently in our long-term memory. In order for our long-term memory to be engaged, our minds must use a process of association and organization to enable the memories to 'stick'. The name for this personal model of organizing information and experience in the mind is a 'schema'.

Mnemonics

Most schemata are personally constructed, and based upon previous experiences. A mnemonic is a schema that is designed by one person for somebody else to use. The single-sentenced fable 'Richard Of York Gave Battle In Vain' is a familiar mnemonic that encodes the sequence of colours of the rainbow; the initial letters match the first letters of the colour sequence red, orange, yellow, green, blue, indigo and violet. Mnemonics, like mental 'zip files', can be useful ways to compress otherwise cryptic information, such as passwords. Musical melodies and jingles can act as mnemonics, helping us to store important phrases or number sequences.

Metaphors

A metaphor is a way of comparing an unfamiliar concept or situation to a familiar one. The computer desktop is a metaphor relating the (initially) new experience of navigating a computer hard disk to the familiar rules of an office workspace. New platforms and experiences will require sensibly constructed metaphors so that users can migrate from the known to the unknown. Metaphors allow the user to apply what they already know, which is easier than memorizing something new.

Usability guru Jakob Nielsen believes that minimizing memory-load is one of the most important features of a user interface design. Users should never have to remember something, or retrace their steps, in order to make sense of what is in front of them.

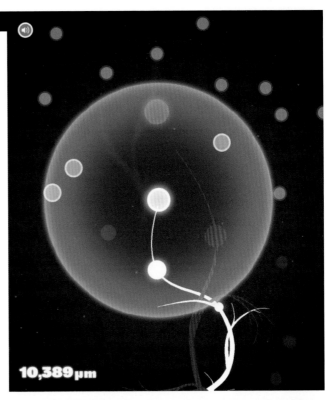

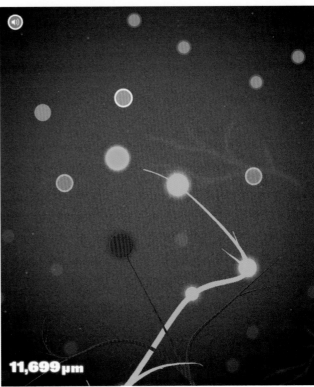

2.6
The goal of Axon
In *Axon*, created for the Wellcome Trust by Preloaded, the player takes on the viewpoint of a neuron inside the brain. The goal of the game is to form long neuron connections by clicking on protein 'targets' within the active circle of influence. The interface of the game is elegantly simple, thus avoiding information overload. The behaviour of 'special' targets, which may accelerate the growth, or increase the circle of influence, is learned as they are encountered. The user has no need to load their memory with complex rules and abstract controls: they just play.

When things go wrong and people have negative experiences, it is tempting to blame the user. But errors are more often the result of a design that misleads, confuses or distracts the user, or which motivates inappropriate behaviour.

Fallibility experts have defined several types of error. A 'slip' occurs when the user plans to act correctly, but inadvertently performs an incorrect action. Slips may be spotted if appropriate feedback mechanisms keep users informed of their actions. The impact of slips can be reduced if the users have the scope to 'undo' their actions.

'Lapses' occur when too many demands are placed on our attention or memory; we plan a correct action but forget to execute it. Lapses can be minimized by use of simplicity and consistency: hierarchy and emphasis in the visual design, for example. Progress indicators and validation procedures can unburden the cognitive load on the user.

A 'mistake' occurs when an incorrect action is planned and faithfully executed. It would be unfair to blame the skill or knowledge of the user for mistakes, because mistakes can occur when there is an expectation gap. For example, when users have been conditioned to act one way, and are suddenly required to break this familiar pattern.

A more wilful error is a 'violation': the user intentionally breaks the rules of a system. A degree of behaviour control is required to avert violations. Careful observation of the users and their contexts may help to better understand their expectations and motivations, and to give some explanation for their actions. In some European cities, the 'Don't Walk' symbol on pedestrian crossings is supplemented by count-down timers to indicate the remaining time until the safe crossing interval. The timers may seem redundant, as the lights change very frequently, and the crossing light symbols are universally understood. But even a short wait can seem like a lifetime if you are in a hurry, and people are fallible, and impatient. The timer discourages them from making opportunistic attempts to cross the road that could result in serious harm.

As the architects of positive experiences, designers should respect that we can all be less than perfect. When things go wrong, the user should be alerted without criticism or condescension. Everybody is fallible, but there are few things more likely to create a negative user experience than being made to feel like a failure.

2.7
The fallibility of human experience
'Plan B' is an app concept by Rona Marin Miller that positively exploits the fallibility of human experience. It provides a context-specific listing of nearby events should the best-laid plans go awry.

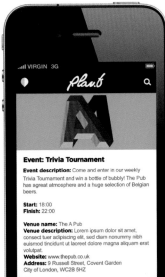

Philosopher Immanuel Kant claimed that a sense of cause and effect is innate; that is, we are born with an expectation that every action has some kind of consequence. Our memories of causes and effects are amassed into a model of the world that shapes our expectations of all future experiences. In general, negative experiences result when reality does not match our mental model of how things respond and develop.

Feedback

We may not expect a kettle to boil water instantaneously, but we do expect immediate confirmation that the 'on' button has been activated. Feedback is a way of acknowledging that an action like this has occurred. Audible feedback may be a mere beep. Visual feedback may be a subtle state-change of a user interface. Feedback can be tactile too: the reassuring 'clunk' of a switch provides feedback that the switching action has been registered.

'Deliver on positive expectations and people experience pleasure. Deliver something different than expected, but equally satisfying, and people have fun.'
– Donald Norman

Closure

One of the most comforting expectations that a user will have is a demand for closure or 'resolution' to denote that the experience is at an end. When a movie ends, the credits roll and the closing music plays; in an online transaction, final confirmation and payment must be acknowledged and confirmed, and delivery information announced. Without clear closure, a user will be left hanging, asking themselves, 'Are we done ...?'

Consistency

Users will reasonably expect similar things to behave in a similar way. Consider the game universe of a first-person shooter game: some doors may be opened and explored, whereas others, due to the boundaries of the game world, are merely surface decoration. There must be a distinct visual difference to these different doors to denote their contrasting behaviour, otherwise the logic of the game world will appear to break down. The same principle can be applied to all types of interfaces and controls.

Confounding expectations

Users may get frustrated if events are not what they expect. However, confounding expectations is not always a bad thing. If the outcome is different to what is expected, but still satisfying, then the result is pleasant surprise; whereas suspense can be created by delaying or withholding an outcome.

50 Hz STROBE
LIGHT ANIMATION

2.8
**Record sleeve designed
by Michael Hansen**
Michael Hansen created this
record sleeve for the music of
modern classical composer
Allan Gravgaard Madsen. The
intricate design also appears on
the surface of the vinyl, which
reveals a kaleidoscope dance of
crystalline shapes and patterns
when played on a turntable
under a strobe light. The record
and packaging provide an
unconventional and unexpected
dimension to the experience
of playing a record, listening to
music or reading cover notes.

Motivation is the influence of inner desires on outward behaviour. Most human behaviour can be attributed to several basic desires or needs, and this can explain what drives people to participate in a sustained experience.

All human beings need acceptance from a peer group, and this requirement can influence our behaviour. In addition, human beings have an underlying appetite to have influence over others: to have status within their own peer group, and to exercise power or vengeance over opposing groups. This may manifest itself as competitive urges in games or status in peer-review forums.

Once status within a group has been achieved, the need to become more individual arises. There may be an appetite for learning for its own sake, or the desire to have an influence over the environment, by organizing or by possessing things. Equally, altruistic forces may take prominence; such as gaining satisfaction from helping others.

The most fundamental human needs are the requirement for food, exercise and safety. If safety is violated, then all other motivating forces vanish. Users must have confidence in the security of their experience; otherwise they will feel fear or anxiety. It is important that experiences should promote a feeling of security and trust, especially if the task relies upon extrinsic motivation.

Extrinsic versus intrinsic motivation

Some experiences contain the rewards for participation, so these are described as intrinsically motivated: the motivation comes from within. Playing games is usually intrinsically motivated, as achievement or progress within the game provides its own rewards. In contrast, completing tax returns is unlikely be intrinsically motivating. In this case, extrinsic (external) forces provide the motivation, such as the fear of penalties or a sense of duty. Similarly, the task of designing a bespoke business card at a self-printing kiosk may be externally motivated by the desire for prestige or status.

In all cases, it is a good idea to consider exactly what will energize a user to perform a task, or to sustain an experience. Designers can incorporate reminders of what is at stake. Progress bars, leader boards, rewards, and even appropriate imagery can all reinforce motivated behaviour.

The action of leaving a web review on goods or services may be motivated by a selfish appetite for status or achievement points, but it can also be motivated by a selfless desire to share and care for others.

2.9

2.9
Cavey toys
Cavey is a series of lovingly
handmade plush toys, each with
their own unique personality.
Analogue created a playful
website for the brand, which
included animations and a fully
integrated story. The vibrant
and colourful gallery of available
Cavey toys appeals to the
users' appetite for collecting; a
fundamental motivating force.
The site integrates with social
media sites so that individual
users' behaviour, their designs
and acquisitions, can gather
approval from a peer group.

Interactive media offers a form of experience in which the user has some control over the system they are using. Often this control involves navigating through content and making choices in order to achieve a goal, such as sending a message or paying for items purchased. The user's progress towards their goal in an interactive system can be thought of as a journey.

A 'user journey' is analogous to one in the physical world, having a starting point and multiple potential routes. Similarly, it is possible to get lost in an interactive system, take a wrong direction or get completely stuck. Unlike a real journey a user can abandon an interactive journey at any point. This can have consequences for websites that rely on their users to complete tasks, such as completing a payment process, and so designers usually need to make a user's journey as smooth as possible.

There are at least three user journey methods in a UXD approach that can be applied to help improve an interactive design:

1. Designers can ask users to *envisage* a journey to help shape an early navigational design.

2. Insights can be derived by *observing* users making journeys through prototypes of the design.

3. Designs can be *analysed* to reveal data about actual user journeys once they are up and running. This live analysis is done by tracking user interactions.

In this activity you will try out methods one and two, envisaging and observing, with the aim of improving the user experience in a small-scale interactive design. Using these methods should minimize any serious problems with user navigation before the design is implemented. Method three, live analysis, allows designers to optimize the user experience based on large amounts of data over significant time periods. It is not possible to use method three without deploying the design, but it is worth noting its existence here because it has the potential to validate the work done through envisaging and observing.

Activity

Requirements

You will need pencil and paper and one or more people to provide their ideas and feedback. For the optional step 4 you will also need access to a computer and basic prototyping software. Flowella is suggested and can be downloaded free from: developer.nokia.com.

Step 1 – create a scenario

If you are working on a project then create a scenario in which a user will use your design to complete a task and achieve a goal. Alternatively create a scenario for an imagined system, for example:

'Thirteen-year-old Gemma is taking part in a nature study and needs help to identify wild birds in her garden, count the number of times she sees them in a day and submit the information to a website.'

Step 2 – ask the user to envisage the journey

Explain the scenario and ask the user to describe how they will approach the task. Depending on the user they may prefer to explain how they would achieve the task in the absence of a fully interactive system. In Gemma's case she may refer to illustrations in a printed guide to identify different wild birds, use a note pad to record when she see a particular type of bird and submit her research to the website by using an online form. As an interactive designer you probably already see the potential for interactive media to improve the user experience for Gemma. For the purpose of this activity the last stage of the task, entering data to the website form, will provide a sufficient challenge to recognize the benefits of creating a user journey. Encourage the user to think freely, without constraints imposed by screens or website pages. Make lots of notes to use in the next step.

Step 3 – visualize the journey

Using pencil and paper turn the user's ideas of the journey into a sequence of sketched frames. For Gemma's journey, from paper notepad to entering data using a web form, visualize each step in the route identifying points at which Gemma can make a choice of direction and show these as branches from the main route. See if you can identify 'break points' where Gemma may take a wrong turn, get stuck or just irritated with the process. Carefully consider what changes could be made to improve the experience. Look for ways to remove the need for the user to repeat tasks such as re-entering data, or looping through multiple steps that could be achieved in one stage.

Step 4 – make the journey (optional)

You may like to create a mock-up of the design using a quick prototype. There are many tools that can link sketch designs by making images (or parts of images) clickable. Flowella, developed by Nokia, is free, easy to use and well supported. Among other features, Flowella creates a graphical view of the available routes a user can take to navigate through the application and this is useful for checking that the routes provided are practical and logical to the user's mind (see fig. 2.11).

Step 5 – observe users making the journey

Sit with one or more users and ask them to make the journey using the sequence of sketched frames or quick prototype as a visual aid. Keep a focus on the original scenario and remind users of their task and goal. Be alert to inevitable user comments such as 'how do I do that?' and 'where do I go now?'. Answer such questions with 'how would you like to do that?' or 'where do you need to go?'.

The activity will be revealing and should result in many suggested changes to the original navigation design. These suggestions need to be recorded so that they are not missed when developing the second iteration of the design.

Activity 2
Observing a user journey

Outcomes

If this activity has been successful then you will have revealed differences between your initial concept of the user journey, the user's envisaged journey and the observed journey. It is likely that you will have identified 'break points' with the potential to alienate the user through poor interaction design. You should recognize that, for relatively little effort, these methods can dramatically improve the user experience when used to help shape interaction designs. They also reduce the risk of poor or failing designs finding their way into the real world and act as insurance against live analysis proving that the initial designs were defective.

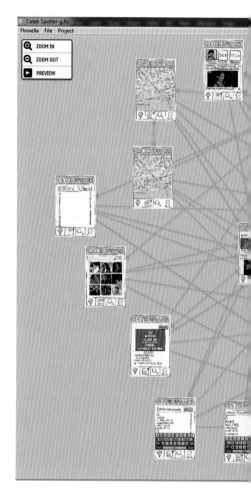

2.10
Flowella
Nokia's Flowella enables designers and developers to create prototype applications using scanned images of hand-sketches to which 'flows' from sketched controls can be defined. The prototype provides a simple way to run user tests and easily make modifications to the design and ultimately to improve the quality of the user journey. Here we see an example from the development of the 'Celeb Spotter' app, by Megan Payne.

2.10

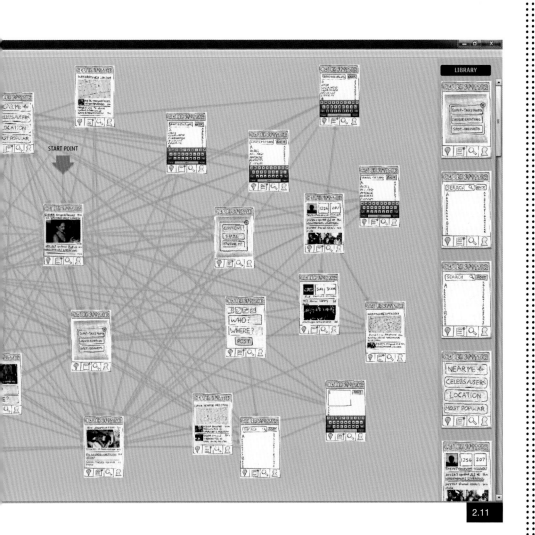

2.11

2.11
Flowella sketch frame
At this point in the user
journey through the 'Celeb
Spotter' application the user is
presented with clear 'signposts'
to complete tasks (enter data
about who and where a photo
was taken) or choose another
'direction' such as visiting a feed
of photos and comments from
other users.

Experience design

Creating a good user experience requires knowledge of the subjective human factors that define them. When users describe an interface as 'intuitive' or 'fun', they are doing so in the context of their own situation and life experience. In this chapter, we discuss some of the more common 'user factors', explain how an understanding of them can inform the decisions that shape a new interactive design, and show how this approach is needed to achieve other benefits, such as competitive advantage and productivity.

Competitive advantage is a term used to describe the characteristics of a product or service that make it more likely to be selected than others in the same market. The characteristics that give products or services competitive advantage include price, availability, design and function. In a market where there is strong competition, products or services that have been around for a while will have reached a point where gaining additional competitive advantage is difficult. After a company has made its product as affordable, available, well designed and functional as they can, what do they do next to improve their competitive advantage?

3.1
Searching, reviewing and licensing music
Lisnmusic is a music search and licensing service that delivers users a seamless experience when searching, reviewing and licensing music. The site competes on the basis of ease-of-use and convenience with the strong advantage of offering instantaneous licensing of chosen tracks. To promote the site, design agency Analogue produced a simple fold out mailer that housed a CD and reflected their cutting edge and forward-thinking approach to music synchronization.

There are times when your client may ask you to justify a UXD approach. You could respond by arguing that designs that deliver a good user experience will be more successful and ultimately more rewarding. In a hard-edged commercial world you will also need to show how a UXD approach can create additional competitive advantage.

It is difficult to quantify the effects of UXD on a specific project's competitive advantage. Here is a question that the client can be asked before the project starts:

'How do you think you can make your product or service more competitive?'

In answering this question, a client is likely to respond with ideas that are directly related to their perspective on the product or service. A typical response may be:

➜ Make it competitively priced

➜ Make it more attractive

➜ Make it provide more functionality.

The same list from a user's point of view would read:

➜ Make it affordable to me

➜ Make it appeal to my aesthetic sense

➜ Make it surprise me with its capability to meet my needs.

A UXD approach can provide clear insights into users that help us deliver what they want. Delivering more of what users want is one way to achieve a new competitive advantage.

3.1

Branding is a marketing tool. In developing a brand, the goal of marketers is to create an attitude in the mind of the consumer towards a product in order to differentiate it from competing goods and services. Branding is a way in which a provider can make a 'promise' to a user, that an experience will deliver recognizable and consistent values. Effective branding can add value to a product or service to the degree that the consumer will pay a premium for that brand.

Companies may reinforce their brand position by sponsoring events that reflect their brand ideals, or by using endorsements from celebrities who typify those ideals. Brand identities are most often upheld by consistently communicating and delivering a user experience that embodies those ideals.

Should the user have any negative experiences associated with the brand, then the brand is tainted and can become devalued. What is more, developing and maintaining a brand can be a very expensive investment for a company. For these reasons, most corporations protect and manage their brand identities very carefully.

Brands are the result of a sustained and informed business strategy and do not emerge overnight. You may find yourself in a position where you are producing work that must conform to brand expectations. By developing a good understanding of the brand you will gain insights into the expectations of the end user.

'Your brand or your name is simply your reputation, you have to fight in life to protect that as it means everything. Nothing is more important.'
– Richard Branson

3.2

3.2
Honouring brand values
The Adidas brand is built
upon a passion for sport and
a sporting lifestyle. Honouring
the brand values was one of
the most important criteria
for design agency Dinosaur
when creating interactive
social games for their
valued customers.

In every area of human life there are different ways to approach tasks and achieve objectives. We recognize productivity as a word used to describe the efficiency of a particular approach to a task. By recording the time taken to complete a task and assessing what has been produced, it is possible to measure levels of productivity. When designing interactive applications, it is useful to consider the user and their need to be productive. It may help to think of the system that you are designing as a tool. High levels of productivity will be achieved if the tool is well matched both to the user and to the task. Subtle changes in the design can make big changes to levels of productivity, particularly when the system is large scale and involves many users.

The relationship between user satisfaction and productivity is complex and will vary depending on the context of the task and the user. If it were possible to design away all the challenges of a task, it would be less satisfying to most users. When an interactive design is thought to be difficult to use, or reduces productivity by requiring needless steps, then this is both unsatisfying and unproductive. Users need well-balanced and flexible designs that allow them to be productive and to gain satisfaction by applying their ability and effort to the best effect.

3.3
Developing creative skills
Screens from an app made by Preloaded for the National Museums of Scotland. The app was designed to help young people develop their creative skills by making their own individual human and animal faces, which could be turned into a mask or poster. By interchanging vibrant heads, eyes, mouths and noses, each encounter offered the user the chance to create something personal and unique.

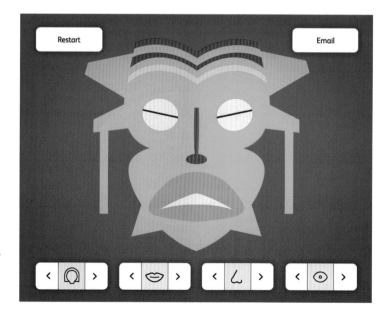

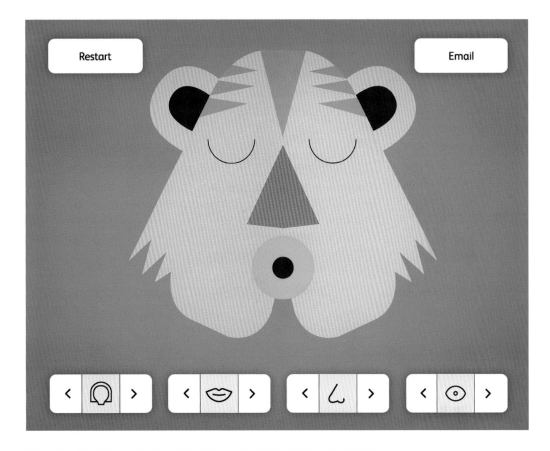

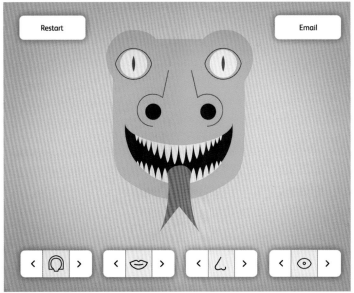

3.3

Chris Atherton is a freelance User Experience Architect.

Chris Atherton is fascinated by human attention, and has a background in behavioural science. In her work for Numiko, Mendeley, the BBC, Skype and others, Chris has applied this expertise to create products that help people learn, make content easier to understand, or create positive social change. Here, Chris explains how user involvement is critical to the UX process, from early research through to prototyping.

First, could you describe what UX designers do?

It is important to describe your company in a way that people – especially prospective customers – are going to understand.

I think a lot of companies get stuck with the term 'web design' because it is broadly correct, and is well understood. But so much of what we do is *not* web design: creating digital strategies, making educational games, storyboarding and making short films, designing mobile applications... all sorts of things. I would say that we build digital tools that help people to learn, live, and communicate better.

How does your expertise in human behaviour help in the early stages of a design process?

My research background in visual perception can come in handy: I'm always interested in what we will be showing users and what effects those visuals might have on their thought and decision-making processes. I've worked with really great design teams, with a really intuitive grasp of what will work and not work on the page. But occasionally, like when we usability test games that have animations, we get into interesting territory around what people notice (or don't notice) — and it's my job to untangle the results and say 'well, psychology would explain this as follows…' and try to improve the user experience according to what I know about human vision and attention.

What is the role of users in a UXD approach?

In a UXD approach, you have to get some kind of concrete feedback from the user. It isn't enough for them to say 'I like it', because what a person *says they like* and what they actually *do* can sometimes be quite different.

I start by finding out who our users are and what they need. This will be aligned with, but not always exactly the same as, the client's business requirements. From there I may work up a content map and information architecture – maybe doing some user card-sorts (see page 150). As soon as there is something users will understand, you can start getting feedback, even if all there is to go off is a simple prototype or some rough sketches.

There is a huge gap between understanding users' behaviour and being able to create good visual design around that, so I'm always interested in how simple prototypes affect the thought- and decision-making processes of the users.

Ideally you would iterate and run usability testing several times during a project, but that depends on several factors, such as the budget or the launch date.

How much of UXD is based on observing or interviewing real people?

My answer to this is always 'not enough'! It is very hard to build a good product if you don't know who it is for, or what they need. And interviewing or usability testing always has the capacity to surprise you: even if you involve only a handful of people, someone will always come at it from a perspective you had not considered. It is definitely a mistake to treat people as if they were some kind of collective who all respond in the same way. We all behave according to our own personal histories – that is quite a hard thing to design for.

What are the 'tools' that allow you to involve the user and their insights?

The tools of my job are:

Card sorting. This is really helpful when you're trying to understand people's expectations around the product's information architecture.

Personas. These are one of the most digestible ways of helping stakeholders to understand how the product is serving the users. If you combine personas with *user journeys*, that can really help to give you a sense of who is interacting with your product, and how.

Usability testing. This might be freeform – where the participant just browses at will – or task-based – where users are asked to achieve something specific, such as buy a product and check out.

Usability recording software. This is used to record your participants while they interact with your prototype. Examples are Silverback or Mora. Mobile apps with similar functionality are emerging too.

Statistics. Statistics can be a good complement to the more qualitative, in-person research end of UXD. With a bit of know-how, you can run statistical tests on anything: website analytics, surveys or the results of usability testing if you have enough participants. Statistics can help to show if the patterns you are seeing are due to chance.

The right attitude. It really, really helps if you are curious about people, and can relate to them one-to-one. If you can make participants comfortable, and get them to talk about themselves and their experiences (but at the same time remain objective and not bias the outcome by asking leading questions), you're on the right track.

What are some of the simplest ways for young designers to consider or involve the user?

Think about the *context* in which people are interacting with your product. Who are they? Are they tired? Busy? What are they trying to do? If you think about UXD as being about the user's journey or task, rather than about, say, a static webpage, your designs will be much more effective.

Try to avoid designing experiences that demand the users' attention in several ways at once, or that rely on users to remember information while they transition from one section to another.

As designers, make mistakes and let the user tell you about them! Generally, the only way you know you have made a mistake is to examine (through analytics or usability testing) the feelings of the people using your product. Can they use it to do what they need to do? Is it nice to use?

3.4

3.4
British Thyroid Foundation Animation
A still from a short video for the British Thyroid Foundation. The aim of the video was specific: to help children recently diagnosed with a thyroid problem understand their condition. The audience however is diverse: the animation had to be clear enough to make sense to a six-year-old, but fun and rapid enough to hold the attention of an older child.

Chris was part of the Numiko team who took an early design – a printed storyboard of the proposed animation– into a primary school. The book was read aloud with some five- and six-year olds, then again with some nine- and ten-year-olds. The prototype was a hit: the kids in both classes loved the story and laughed at the funny bits. They recalled the story, successfully retaining all the technical information, and provided valuable feedback to the design team, such as to make the doctor a bit more reassuring in the final animation.

Fun is a difficult concept to define. 'Fun' can have connotations of triviality and frivolity, but fun operates on a much more meaningful level if the goal is to provide true value to users.

Fun and discovery

Fun usually involves some kind of discovery: recognizing something unusual, but reconciling it with our understanding of the rules of a system. Fun belongs to the part of our nature that desires challenge and growth as well as order and security.

Gestalt theory shows us that humans are reassured by patterns. The more we can make sense of things, and organize them, the more secure we feel. But once a pattern is identified, it can become repetitive and boring. We are naturally inquisitive, and seek out new places, new situations, and new patterns to expand our world-view. Interaction is – or should be – intrinsically fun, because interacting with other people or with our environment is the primary way of exploring and discovering.

For a baby, the game of peek-a-boo is fun. The baby is at a stage of development where a new understanding of object permanence is emerging, and there is joy to be had in learning that things still exist in the world, even when they disappear from view.

For an older child, it may be tremendous fun to press a button for a lift or a pedestrian crossing. The joy of being a cause to an effect is a gratifying system of discovery that gives them a new insight into their place in the world. As we grow older and become more self-aware, we strive to achieve some mastery in controlling our environment, whether this is customizing our Facebook page, climbing a mountain or completing the next level of a computer game.

Fun and 'leisure'

Mihaly Czikszentmihalyi, an expert in fun and fulfilment, warns against confusing fun with 'leisure'. Leisure describes a type of consumption which may not necessarily be that rewarding. Fun, on the other hand, is driven by personal satisfaction.

The craft of designing 'fun' lies in the ability to balance what is familiar with what is uncertain. Fun is not something that is bolted on to an experience in the form of silly music, cute characters or dazzling visuals. Fun is an integral part of an experience that relies upon understanding the expectations, motivations and abilities of the user.

3.5

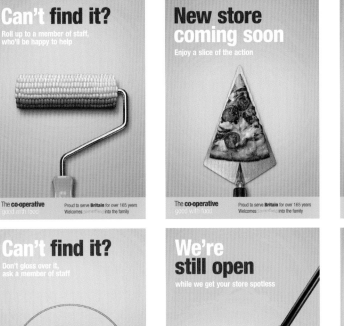

Can't find it?
Roll up to a member of staff,
who'll be happy to help

New store coming soon
Enjoy a slice of the action

We're still open
while we give your store
a lick of paint

The **co-operative** good with food · Proud to serve **Britain** for over 165 years · Welcomes something into the family

The **co-operative** good with food · Proud to serve **Britain** for over 165 years · Welcomes something into the family

The **co-operative** good with food · Proud to serve **Britain** for over 165 years · Welcomes something into the family

Can't find it?
Don't gloss over it,
ask a member of staff

We're still open
while we get your store spotless

New store coming soon
We're just fixing up the store

The **co-operative** good with food · Proud to serve **Britain** for over 165 years · Welcomes something into the family

The **co-operative** good with food · Proud to serve **Britain** for over 165 years · Welcomes something into the family

The **co-operative** good with food · Proud to serve **Britain** for over 165 years · Welcomes something into the family

3.5
Creating visual parallels
In-store improvements and
building works can certainly
undermine the experience
of shopping. Design agency
Dinosaur have mitigated
the disruption to shoppers
with some witty posters for
the Co-operative chain of
supermarkets. The posters
create visual parallels between
the tools of the building trade
and the food on sale.

Usability is a measure of how easily a user can achieve a goal such as entering a building, filling a bathtub with water or ordering a pizza online. It is a subjective measure because levels of usability depend on the user and the context of use. It is also a comparative measure because it aims to compare levels of usability in different designs that attempt to achieve the same goal for users.

Usability testing is carried out to find the functional effectiveness of designs without considering the wider user experience. It is important that designs work for users in a practical and efficient way, but it is also important to recognize that usability methods are just one tool in the design process. Designers need to balance the user's need for stimulation, challenge, discovery and fun against utility and conformity.

3.6

For more information please visit www.bbc.co.uk/21cc

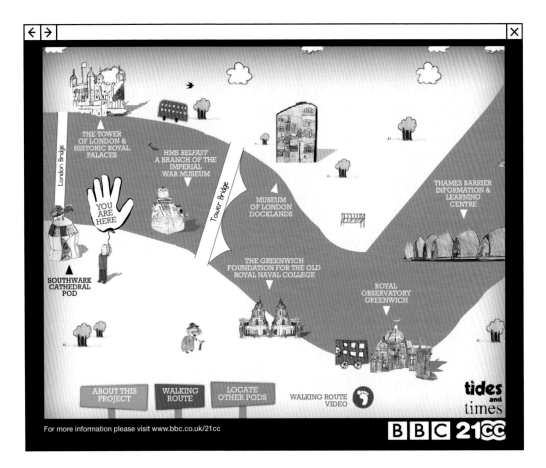

← → | | X

THE TOWER
OF LONDON &
HISTORIC ROYAL
PALACES

London Bridge

HMS *BELFAST*
A BRANCH OF THE
IMPERIAL
WAR MUSEUM

Tower Bridge

MUSEUM
OF LONDON
DOCKLANDS

THAMES BARRIER
INFORMATION &
LEARNING
CENTRE

YOU
ARE
HERE

SOUTHWARK
CATHEDRAL
POD

THE GREENWICH
FOUNDATION FOR THE OLD
ROYAL NAVAL COLLEGE

ROYAL
OBSERVATORY
GREENWICH

ABOUT THIS
PROJECT

WALKING
ROUTE

LOCATE
OTHER PODS

WALKING ROUTE
VIDEO

tides
and
times

For more information please visit www.bbc.co.uk/21cc

BBC 21cc

3.6
Interacting with technology

Maek designed three intriguing touch-screen kiosks for BBC learning, which were situated on a walking route beside the River Thames in London, UK.

A website, inspired by children's drawings, was also developed to support the kiosks.

Adults may not think that the website has anything resembling an interface, but the young target user may think differently, recognizing all the invitations to touch, interact, listen and explore.

Simplicity is a virtue beloved of designers in all disciplines. When applied sensitively and intelligently, simplicity eases the load on the user's memory and attention.

There are several ways in which experiences can be simplified: context menus are a common way of accessing timely features; a 'recent places' or 'last played' option is sensitive to the user's usual behaviour; geo-location technology has empowered some devices to make assumptions about users' needs and wants. But for some users, these simplifications are presumptions that threaten privacy and undermine an experience.

Advocates of simplicity often mistakenly believe that any feature that does not aid functionality and usability is redundant and should be purged. But we should not mistake the principle of simplicity for a mission of sparse minimalism. Aesthetics have a purpose: they contribute to the overall experience. They may be what makes the difference between a usable experience and an enjoyable one.

It may be more useful to think of simplicity as the intelligent management of complexity. When users demand simplicity, they are really asking for sensitivity to their present goals and needs. Simplicity does not mean reducing opportunities for interactions: it means framing these opportunities within a relevant and consistent schema.

But how and when can the end user prioritize their needs and impose relevant schemata on an experience? A UXD approach would be to involve the users as early as possible, and as frequently as possible in the iterative design process.

'Perfection is achieved, not when there is nothing more to add, but when there is nothing left to take away.'
– Antoine de Saint-Exupéry

3.7
The portfolio website of A and R
The beautiful images of Gustav Papeleo require no extra words or widgets to impress. The portfolio website of A and R, which includes the work of Papeleo and other photographers, has an elegant and minimalistic simplicity that allows the images to take centre stage. Lengthy prose, or intrusive navigation, would detract from the amazing body of work on show.

Challenge is a highly subjective part of an experience. A colouring book represents a challenge to a child, because their manual dexterity and colour perception is still developing and their chances of success in the endeavour are as likely as failure. Satisfying experiences are those that recognize and accommodate the evolving skills of the user, and in return present them with appropriate and achievable challenges.

Such experiences provide the user with a realistic opportunity for mastery, and this is a highly motivating force.

When the opportunity for mastery is in a perfectly attuned balance with the degree of challenge, then the user may enter a state called 'flow'. A 'flow' state is so absorbing that we lose all sense of time and purpose, and the task becomes intrinsically motivating: participation is its own reward. A state of flow can be achieved by reading an absorbing book, by playing a musical instrument, or by engaging in extreme sports.

There are several factors that create the potential for flow. It is important that the goals of the task are clear, but it is also crucial that the user receives feedback to assess how comfortably they are developing the skills required to meet imminent challenges. Games have obvious mechanisms that evolve to challenge the evolving competence of the player. But other experiences can utilize the principles of challenges to engage a user.

Feedback

Learning the piano has the potential for flow, because we receive constant and immediate feedback on our progress: we can hear at once if we have played the correct note at the right moment, and can adjust our performance accordingly if an error is made. Conversely, some experiences do not provide the immediate reassurance that our actions – if not wholly successful – are within a margin of manageable failure. These are the experiences that we abandon out of frustration.

3.8
A game providing feedback
The *Launchball* game, designed by Preloaded for the Science Museum in London. Players have an inventory of tiles, each with a characteristic behaviour, such as magnetism, heat or insulation. When arranged correctly, the tiles create powered arrays that propel a ball towards a target. The stages of the game are progressively more challenging, but the game provides frequent feedback and hints to guide the player towards a rewarding solution. The levels of the game are organized according to the increasing skill level of the player, and previous successes are recorded so that the player is aware of their competence.

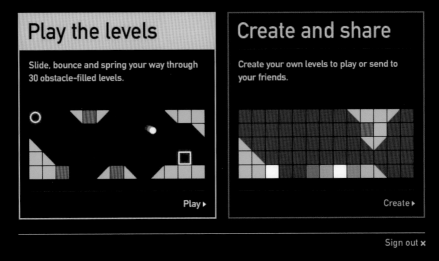

Launchball

Bringing Launchpad online

Play the levels

Slide, bounce and spring your way through 30 obstacle-filled levels.

Play ▸

Create and share

Create your own levels to play or send to your friends.

Create ▸

Sign out ✕

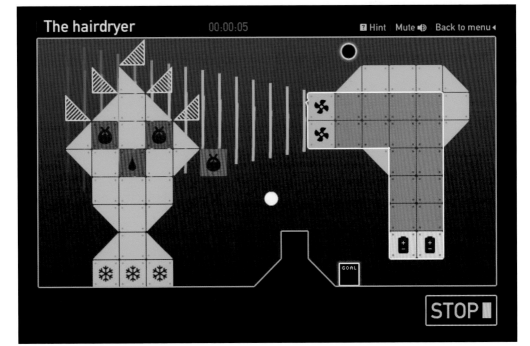

Intuition

It is generally considered high praise for an interactive design to be described as 'intuitive' by its users. The label 'intuitive' implies ease of use and logical operation that does not require the user to think. In fact it is the user who is being intuitive, somehow knowing what to do in specific contexts when presented with a range of interaction choices. The designer has cleverly identified elements of the user's subconscious understanding of visual signs and processes.

It has been said that 'the only intuitive interface is the nipple' and that our lives from birth provide us with experiences that help us develop intuitive understanding that we can apply in different situations. If this is true then designers can expect different intuitive responses from users with different life experiences. Unfortunately this means that a user interface that some find intuitive, others will find unintuitive. In this activity you will aim to recognize intuition similarity (or variation) between two or more users.

> **'Intuition (is) perception via the unconscious.'**
> – Carl Gustav Jung

Activity

You will need plain paper, squared paper, scissors, a camera and at least two people to provide the user data (User A and User B). The activity can be extended for use with a wider range of users.

Step 1
Define an interface 'canvas' with a sheet of squared paper (10mm/0.4" squares are ideal). Users need to know that this represents the 'screen' of the interactive device for example a tablet or desktop computer.

Step 2
Create 12 interface elements out of paper, each measuring 50 x 10mm/2" x 0.4". Write one of the titles from the list below on each element. Add a small arrow on elements that will typically take up a larger area than the paper element itself. User can decide how much extra space to allow (see figure 3.9).

➔ Search

➔ My account

➔ Departments

➔ Buy

➔ Price

➔ Sign-in

➔ Choose quantity

➔ Contact us

➔ Sale feature product

➔ Product photograph

➔ Customer reviews

➔ Product description

Step 3

Making sure that User B is not able to observe or hear this step, ask User A to place each interface element on the squared paper in a position where they would intuitively expect to find it when visiting an online store. You will need to explain that the sheet of squared paper represents the 'screen' and the arrows on some elements mean that they need extra space (see figure 3.10).

Step 4

When all the elements are in place take a photo of the 'screen', so that you have a record of the arrangement. Before removing the elements, draw a pencil outline around each one (see figure 3.11).

Step 5

Provide User B with the paper interface elements and ask them to place each interface element on the canvas inside one of the pencil outlines. They should position them in the space closest to where they would intuitively expect to find them when visiting an online store.

Step 6

When User B has placed all the interface elements in position use the photo taken in step 4 to identify differences between the layout created by each user.

Step 7

Discuss any differences in the choice of element layout with the two users. If the layout arrangements appear substantially different then continue testing with more users to build a better understanding of different intuitive responses. If the differences are slight, then the design already has some chance of success.

Outcomes

If this activity has been successful then you will have identified any differences in the intuitive response of the two users. Where conflicts do exist these could be reduced by applying cues that are intuitive to both users, such as the use of scale and colour to create a visual hierarchy. Even a relatively minor change in visual design has the potential to change the user experience. Following the launch of a new interactive web design it is possible to carry out A-B testing. This is a technique where a percentage of visitors are automatically redirected to slightly different versions of the same website and their actions are monitored.

3.9

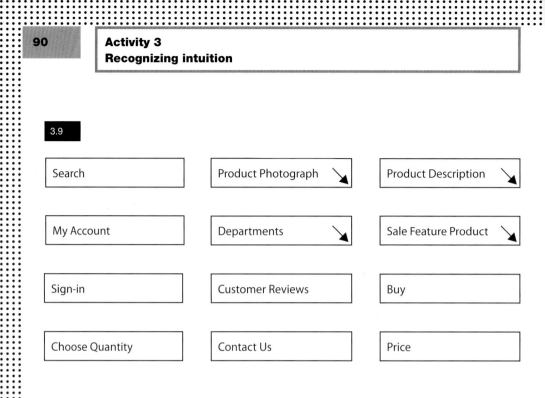

Search

Product Photograph

Product Description

My Account

Departments

Sale Feature Product

Sign-in

Customer Reviews

Buy

Choose Quantity

Contact Us

Price

3.10

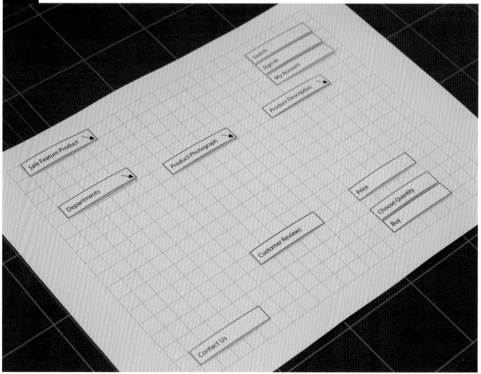

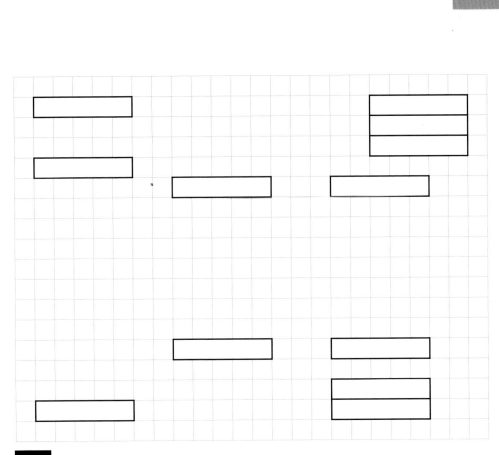

3.11

3.9
Interface elements
The 12 interface elements
ready to be copied in step 2
of the exercise.

3.10
User A's arrangement
A photo taken after User A has
arranged the elements in step 4.

3.11
Canvas with outlines
The canvas with outlines
in which User B must
place the elements in
step 5 of the exercise.

Gestalt is a field of psychology that is concerned with how humans make sense of the world around them. Gestalt psychologists are interested in how the mind organizes and groups together sensory information that appears to be similar or related. A large amount of work has been done to understand how we make sense of complex visual information. As far as gestalt psychologists are concerned, we do not perceive experiences as collections of separate fragments, but *holistically,* meaning 'as a whole'.

An understanding of the gestalt principles of visual perception can help the designer create work that influences user behaviour, so that their navigation through a designed experience feels intuitive and rewarding.

Six principles of gestalt

For many years now, psychologists have accepted that there are six cognitive principles at work when we encounter visual elements in a group. The six principles are potential 'tools' that can influence our arrangement of visual information in a design. Alternatively, the principles may help diagnose how and why visual information is misinterpreted by users. These principles are illustrated in the coming pages and are: closure, continuity, similarity, common fate, figure and ground, and proximity.

3.12
Gestalt principle of proximity
The menu for the Portobello Star is an eclectic mix of maps, calendars and nostalgic typefaces and images. The design is organized in accordance with the gestalt principle of proximity (related sections are grouped, and separated by negative space) and of similarity (the simple colour scheme and consistent character of type and image), which unify the otherwise disparate elements.

3.12

3.13

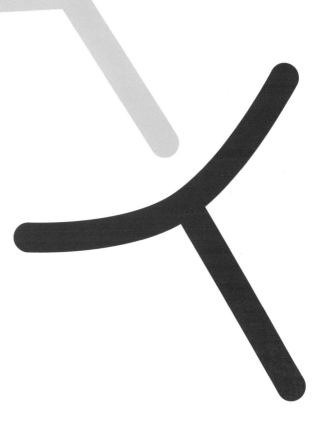

3.13
Closure

The mind is uneasy with images that appear to be incomplete, and will do the extra mental work required to discern closed shapes or patterns. Although these two cards and the background patterns are not delineated with borders, visual closure occurs so that we perceive the image as two stacked cards that are separated from the white stripes behind them, rather than as a single irregular white block attached to several 'combs' of attached white.

3.14
Continuity

The blue 'Y' shape on the top is perceived as three lines joining in the middle. The red 'Y' shape below it, although similar, is perceived as two lines – a curved platform supported by a single stem – because of our inclination to see continuous lines rather than broken or adjoined lines.

3.15

3.15
Similarity
Objects which look similar are regarded as a group, even if they are not adjacent. The 'lemons' above are scattered across the frame, but they are connected by their similarity.

3.16
Common fate
This principle concerns objects that are moving or appear to have direction. When objects share a common movement or direction, they are perceived as grouped. The figures above appear to share a common path, so they are perceived as either one figure at different stages of a fall, or several figures that are understood to imminently fall.

3.17
Figure & ground
When we perceive objects to be 'stacked' one above the other, we are making figure and ground judgments. The image above is perceived as a yellow circle on top of a white blob on top of blue circle (or a fried egg on a plate).

3.18
Proximity
Objects that are close to each other are perceived to be related. The distribution of white space in this image suggests that this is three groups of car symbols, rather than nineteen separate symbols.

3.18

Communication is accomplished via the exchange of small 'parcels' of meaning called 'signs'. Signs may take the form of spoken words and sounds; of graphical images and symbols; or they may take the form of gestures, or body language.

Users are active seekers and decoders of signs. Everything and anything can be assumed to carry meaning: even a blank screen is a sign (usually a sign that something has gone wrong). Semiotics is the branch of communication studies that is concerned with the relationship between signs and meaning, and it can provide us with insights into the opportunities for efficient communications, as well as warn us of potential miscommunication.

Certain types of sign are extremely arbitrary: that is, they rely upon a shared code in which a sign 'stands for' something else, just as a green light in many cultures denotes 'go'. These arbitrary signs are called 'symbols', and are based on a principle of mutual understanding that has evolved or been negotiated between everybody involved in the communication process. Consequently, symbols are highly coded, meaning simply that if you don't know the rules of the sign-system, you can't understand the message. Symbols which are well-known to designers and programmers may be part of a specific, acquired literacy that is unfamiliar to other people.

Icons and indexes are less arbitrary, more intuitive types of signs. It is possible to infer the meaning of an index or icon without prior knowledge of a shared code, because an icon has a visual similarity with the thing it represents, whereas an index has an alternative relationship with the thing it signifies (for example, a 'causal' relationship). Three vertical wavy lines could, in the context of a shower-tap, indicate 'hot water'. The lines may have an 'iconic' resemblance to rising water vapour, but the cause-effect relationship between the sign and what it means has an indexical link: 'water vapour will rise because the water is hot'.

Constructing meaning from signs can be taxing on memory and attention, and may demotivate users. On the other hand, recognizing the 'language' of a new experience, particularly a novel technology, may be a part of the intrinsic pleasure of the experience.

3.19
Linkem, a bespoke visual language

Linkem is a deceptively simple but engrossing game about making strong connections. The goal is to strategically place different disks that cause their neighbours to change their behaviour, strengthening or weakening the links between them.

The team at Preloaded designed a custom visual alphabet of seven different disk symbols. Each symbol has a singular, predictable behaviour. The user has to learn these behaviours very quickly in order to place the disks in the optimum sequence. The simple, unified orange-and-white patterns of the disks belie the sophistication of the bespoke visual language that Preloaded have created.

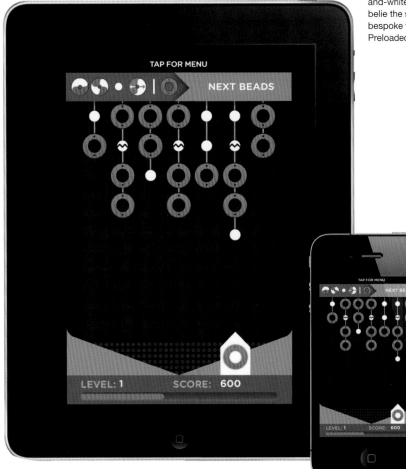

Experience is continuous. *An* **experience is different: an experience has a beginning, a middle and an end. In order to define, recount and evaluate experiences, we need some way to delineate these from the constant flow of sensory experience.**

Story

Story is one of the most fundamental ways in which we can mentally partition our experiences. The rules of systems that we use to organize events into meaningful and engaging stories is called 'narrative', and an understanding of narrative is ingrained in all users, even if they are not conscious of the structure. All previous experiences have shaped our expectations, and for thousands of years the principles of classical narrative have been observed in storytelling, literature and theatre.

Features

There are several features of a fully realized narrative:

➔ *A protagonist:* a 'hero' or 'heroine' with a sense of purpose.

➔ *A goal:* treasure to be found; justice to be served; order to be restored; love to be won.

➔ *A force of antagonism:* a 'bad-guy' that gets in the way; a natural or supernatural force that provides conflict; a trait or flaw that threatens the hero's capabilities.

➔ *Causality:* a pattern of cause-and-effect in which the protagonist is an agent of change; things happen (desirable or not) because of the hero/heroine's efforts.

➔ *Resolution:* a positive outcome; balance is restored to the universe of the protagonist.

These elements form the obvious structure of most novels and movies, as well as providing the underlying motivational logic of many games. But narrative is a structure that could be applied to many other interactive experiences.

Commitment

Some experiences require a degree of orientation before the user feels fully committed: this corresponds to the 'equilibrium' that begins a story. Once the user is committed to the task at hand, the narrative journey is underway.

We can regard users as the protagonists of their own experience. They have a goal to accomplish, and may reasonably view the process of achieving this as a series of obstacles to be overcome. Users will regard themselves as the agent responsible for change, so we should do as much as possible to create the feeling that goals are achievable and actions are effective. When the goal has been fulfilled, the user should sense that balance has been restored: that their efforts have been fully resolved.

If we provide a user with a sense of where they are in their own narrative journey, they will be better orientated and motivated to proceed. By imposing or suggesting a narrative structure, we can make an experience more discrete and memorable.

3.20

www.blabla.nfb.ca

3.20
Interactive media
Bla Bla is an interactive
animated film created by
Vincent Morisset. As with
conventional narrative films,
the story plays through several
scenes in a fixed sequence;
each scene visually exploring
a different principle of human
communication. Unlike
traditional films, the viewer can
interact with the characters,
provoking them into speech,
argument, or silence.

A constraint is a consciously engineered part of an interactive experience that is designed to limit or influence user behaviour. Constraints may protect the user against harm, or error, or they may be part of the 'instruction' required to make sense of the experience.

What are constraints?

Constraints are important tools for managing user expectations and minimizing user frustration. A client-sided script that validates an email address; a 'wizard' that prescribes the sequence and scope of interactions; a 'warning' dialogue; these are all constraints designed to spare the user wasted time and effort.

3.21
West Hill Primary School
At West Hill Primary School, playful signage invites the children to 'feed' items into their rightful storage spaces, and vibrant floor patterns encourage the children to sit in an orderly fashion. In products and interactive applications as well as environments, subtle constraints like these can influence user behaviour without being forceful or overbearing.

Problems with constraints

However, a poorly conceived constraint may add to frustration and dissatisfaction. Constraints should match the users' mental concept of what is and is not permitted. Where constraints are imposed, the reasons should be transparent and consistent. If a user feels that they are being denied legitimate choices, or admonished for legitimate actions, they may feel dissatisfied. A customer may be justifiably prevented from adding two-and-a-half tins of soup to their basket, but may feel frustrated if two-and-a-half kilos/pounds of tomatoes is not an acceptable choice.

The degree of constraint should also be proportional to the potential for error or harm. A 'no exit' sign is a constraint that discourages leaving by the wrong door. A turnstile does the same thing more forcibly.

Users accept and can even appreciate constraints. Often, constraints are there for reasons of safety and influence; sometimes they are imposed to create a challenge. The game of chess would be much simpler, but much less fun, if all the pieces moved in all directions. It is because of the constraints that the user finds opportunities for learning and mastery which, if applied consistently and fairly, enhance an experience rather than diminish it.

3.21

Design process

The products of a UXD approach are analogous to a theatre show. When it begins, the audience expects entertainment. Oblivious to what has gone on prior to the performance, they expect a fulfilling experience. In the theatre, a bad show may be seen by hundreds. On the Web, bad interactive design may be seen (and used) by millions.

Here, we look at the processes needed to manage and deliver effective UXD. We look at the life cycle of a design and how user research and participation helps shape the design specification. These activities can be time-consuming and costly, hence we introduce techniques to manage the process. In conclusion, we aim to show that good process leads to better designs.

The phrase 'project life cycle' tends to imply a straightforward journey through the project from start to completion. In reality there will be more than one thing happening at the same time and some tasks will be repeated until the output from them is satisfactory. Some aspects of the life cycle will be concrete and measurable and others will be abstract and require judgement made on the basis of evidence-based research. The process is tricky to describe in words and so graphics are often used to visualize the life cycle and make a complex project structure easier to understand.

That said, it is possible to identify specific actions that are common to a UXD approach:

➜ the creation of a concept brief that will outline a strategy and include the project scope and objectives;

➜ the bringing together of a multidisciplinary design team;

➜ the identification of users and their needs, including the tasks and environments of the design;

➜ user research, including an understanding of the environment in which users will experience the design and how the design addresses the whole user experience;

➜ initial design and development of one or more creative approaches;

➜ user-centred evaluation followed by design selection and refinement;

➜ further user evaluation until satisfactory evaluation results are achieved;

➜ deployment of the design and continuous evaluation in its live state.

4.1
Preloaded publishing strategy
The education department of UK broadcaster Channel 4 commissioned Preloaded to create *Supersight*, an innovative, cross-platform game imbued with key learning messages of resilience, self-determination and control. One of the most important requirements of the brief was to identify where in the world the game was being played, as well as to iterate and improve based on player feedback.

As part of the planned life cycle of a game, Preloaded schedule releases carefully, and use Google Analytics to track the download locations of games. They aim to get good editorial coverage of games, and converse with users of online gaming portals, setting aside time for reactive tweaks in the first few weeks following a release.

4.1

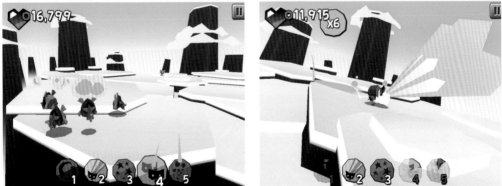

In Chapter 2, we briefly introduced the concept of user research and the identification of target users and their goals in using an interactive system. Good user research is needed to inform the design process, answering fundamental questions such as:

➜ Who are the users?

➜ What are the users' goals?

➜ In what context will the system be used?

The process

The design team will interpret the information gained through user research to develop a list of user requirements and generate initial design ideas. The process of interpreting user research is the first stage in an iterative design process. Iteration in this context means that the design is evaluated, the evaluation triggers improvements in the design, and then the design is evaluated again. This loop continues until the design is demonstrated to provide a good user experience that allows the target user group to achieve the required goals in specific contexts.

'Iteration should be used to progressively eliminate uncertainty during the development of interactive systems. Iteration implies that descriptions, specifications and prototypes are revised and refined when new information is obtained in order to minimize the risk of the system under development failing to meet user requirements.'
– *The International Standard ISO 9241-210:2010*

Evaluation

One way to evaluate a design is through user feedback and this is best done face-to-face, although there are many different ways that users can be involved. These range from participating in design meetings to being observed while interacting with design prototypes.

In fact there are two loops going on in the design process: the feedback loop and the design iteration loop. Improvements in design are dependent on the methods of evaluation applied and the insights that they produce. Involving users in a constructive feedback is an effective way to provide the information needed to push the design process forward to successful completion.

The credibility of the design team is strengthened by carefully managed user involvement. For the feedback to be valid and useful it needs to be intelligently assessed in relation to the originally defined target users and their goals. The design team needs to prevent user involvement from shifting the design focus by, for example, adding features that are not required to achieve the user's goal.

Designing for human–computer interaction is exceptionally complicated and should probably be classed as exploration rather than design. As in any expedition to explore unchartered territory, it is a good idea to stop every so often, assess progress and confirm that you are heading in the right direction. If the design team were to do this too often then the project's progress would be slow and potentially disrupted by too many changes of direction. If done too infrequently, then the project risks being committed to a direction that cannot be changed due to the amount of work that would need to be undone and the time taken to back-track.

The key to deciding on when to iterate is the availability of new information coming from sources such as user research, technical reports or prototype testing. This implies that activities that generate this information are happening in parallel with the design activity – and so they should. The UXD lead on any project needs to be the lookout in the team, metaphorically running to the top of each hill to survey the horizon and identifying when a change in direction should be considered.

4.2

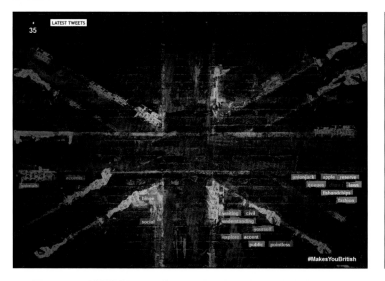

4.2
Harvesting keywords
'Make Bradford British' was a series by British broadcaster Channel 4, which explored identity and nationality. The series was accompanied by a microsite with quizzes and interactive elements. Numiko created an application to harvest keywords tweeted by viewers during and after the broadcast, who could then see the words constructed into a dynamic Union flag.

The activity in Chapter 1 (see page 36) is designed to reveal that designing for a diverse group of users in a range of situations is not an effective approach. In trying to create an interactive design that 'works for everyone, everywhere', a design team is most likely to create something that 'doesn't work very well for anyone, anywhere'. This is because the need to accommodate such broad requirements will result in either too much complexity or too little functionality in the design.

A better tactic is to target a small group of individual users located in appropriate contexts and to design just for them. In this way it is possible to focus on accommodating user characteristics that are similar. This approach makes the design task much less complex and the goal of creating a good user experience for the defined group much more achievable. Interestingly, the results of this approach often give an acceptable user experience to a much more diverse group than the target group defined by the design team.

What is a persona?

A persona is a fictional description of a model user based on high-quality user research of actual users in the target user group. It will include details about the user's education, lifestyle, interests, values, attitudes and patterns of behaviour. The persona will have a name too, allowing the design team to ask each other questions like, 'When does Sally have time to check her email?'

To allow for a range of users within the target group, it is generally considered necessary to create a number of personas (usually fewer than six). This allows the design team to consider differing characteristics such as aptitude, motivation and the context in which the interactive design will be used. Sometimes it may be useful to create personas of people who are not users but who are affected by the design. An example of this could be a parent who may be interested in the educational value of an interactive game for their child.

4.3
Personas as a design tool
The Terence Higgins Trust is a charity that fights to promote good sexual health in order to minimize the spread of HIV and other sexually transmitted infections. The 'Young and Free' microsite, created by Reading Room, is part of a campaign to encourage young people to undertake free Chlamydia testing. Without a clear understanding of the user, the website would have risked embarrassing, confusing or alarming the target demographic. As a design tool, personas – fictitious personalities that represent the typical users of a product or service – act as a useful reminder of who a site like this is for.

4.3

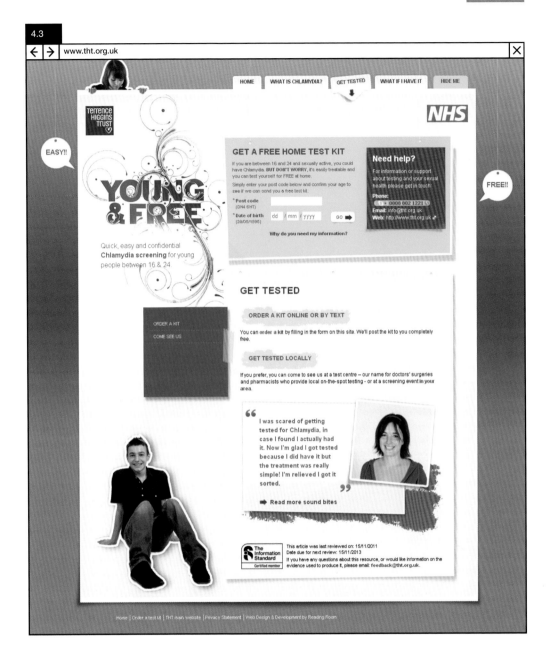

www.tht.org.uk

HOME | WHAT IS CHLAMYDIA? | GET TESTED | WHAT IF I HAVE IT | HIDE ME

EASY!!

FREE!!

YOUNG & FREE

Quick, easy and confidential
Chlamydia screening for young people between 16 & 24

GET A FREE HOME TEST KIT

If you are between 16 and 24 and sexually active, you could have Chlamydia. **BUT DON'T WORRY**, it's easily treatable and you can test yourself for FREE at home.

Simply enter your post code below and confirm your age to see if we can send you a free test kit.

* Post code
(DN4 6HT)

* Date of birth   dd / mm / yyyy   GO ➡
(28/05/1996)

Why do you need my information?

Need help?

For information or support about testing and your sexual health please get in touch

Phone:
0808 802 1221
Email: info@tht.org.uk
Web: http://www.tht.org.uk

GET TESTED

ORDER A KIT ONLINE OR BY TEXT

You can order a kit by filling in the form on this site. We'll post the kit to you completely free.

GET TESTED LOCALLY

If you prefer, you can come to see us at a test centre – our name for doctors' surgeries and pharmacists who provide local on-the-spot testing - or at a screening event in your area.

ORDER A KIT
COME SEE US

" I was scared of getting tested for Chlamydia, in case I found I actually had it. Now I'm glad I got tested because I did have it but the treatment was really simple! I'm relieved I got it sorted. "

➡ Read more sound bites

The Information Standard
Certified member

This article was last reviewed on: 15/11/2011
Date due for next review: 15/11/2013
If you have any questions about this resource, or would like information on the evidence used to produce it, please email: feedback@tht.org.uk.

Home | Order a test kit | THT main website | Privacy Statement | Web Design & Development by Reading Room

4.4

The Cake Baker

Fiona Sterling - 35 year old, owns her own small cake store in Birkdale, UK.

Personal background

Five years ago Fiona started Earth Cake, a new organic cake store just around the corner from her home in Birkdale. Before opening the store her husband of 10 years (Scott) renovated the building and installed all the shop fittings. Scott has worked for a local building firm since leaving college. They both juggle their jobs around looking after their two children, Jessica (12 years) and Sophie (eight years).

Due to to her busy lifestyle, Fiona finds it difficult to find the time to update Earth Cake's social media. When not working on her business, Fiona meets-up with a wide circle of friends who she has known for over 20 years. At home she relaxes with her husband watching evening television and reading historical novels.

Earth Cake is slowly becoming more popular with sales increasing every year. Fiona sometimes has difficulty fulfilling customer requirements for extravagant cake designs. She struggles to find out exactly what cake designs customers want. Discussing options with customers can be very time consuming, taking Fiona away from the production side of the business.

Fiona is looking for a website or application where customers can select or create designs and submit orders easily and quickly. She thinks that this will help grow her business.

User goals

1. To find out what designs her customers want

2. To receive the customers design ideas easily and quickly

3. To advertise the store and company to local people

4. To view other local cake and baking companies

Engagement and activities

Home computer: Fiona shares a computer with the whole family which she uses for around an hour every day.

Internet usage: Fiona uses the Web to read cake forums such as 'Cake Central' and often posts replies to members' questions.

Social media: Fiona uses social media to help promote her cake store on Facebook and Twitter and also has her own personal accounts.

Mobile: Fiona uses a Samsung android phone which she has had for nine months on contract. Fiona makes call rather than sending texts and has just started to use the Facebook app.

Television shows: Fiona spends around four hours a week watching her favourite TV programmes: Cake Boss, Biggest Loser, Dallas.

4.4
Developing a common understanding
User personas help the design team to develop a common understanding of the target user group and to empathize with their needs.

The Cake Enthusiast

Dareia - 28 year old homemaker living in Liverpool, UK.

Personal background

Dareia is originally from Iran, moving to Liverpool with her family at the age of 3. After completing her education in local schools she relocated to London and studied for a degree in Journalism. She has now returned to Liverpool and works part-time writing a lifestyle column for a Manchester newspaper.

Dareia met her husband, an insurance analyst, while working at *The Times* newspaper in London. They have a son, Jake and a Bedlington Terrier puppy called Tinto.

Cake designing is Dareia's main interest outside her family and work. She likes creating ideas for cakes and has a small following of clients and friends who commission her to produce cake designs for different events. Although Dareia is a good cook she prefers her cakes to be made by professional cake bakers. She has a group of close friends and family who meet-up regularly at her home to try new cakes from different companies.

Dareia is looking for a smartphone application that will let her easily find local cake companies, read about baking techniques and meet new friends with similar interests.

User goals

1. To find cake companies who are local to her

2. To easily contact and send her cake requests to companies

3. To learn new baking recipes and techniques

4. To make friends with people who have similar interests in cake design

Engagement and activities

Personal laptop: Dareia regularly uses the Web in the evening to update her personal blog and to research cake designs. Dareia also uses her iPad and iPhone to engage with cake forums, such as 'Cake craft world', often posting and talking to members.

Social media: Dareia keeps a close eye on Facebook to see what her friends and family are doing.

Mobile: Dareia has the latest iPhone model which she uses mainly for sending text messages and keeping in touch with friends and work contacts. She uses an app to record interviews for her column and has a large collection of cake photos, which she uses as reference when creating new designs.

Television shows: Dareia will normally record TV shows on the home PVR to watch later. She enjoys British period drama series and stand-up comedy shows.

Personas can be given life by creating scenarios that feature them in the role of a user. Scenarios are created by the design team to help them see the world from the user's perspective and can start simply and develop in detail as the project progresses. They are useful because they allow the design team to place their ideas in context and to develop functionality that will meet the needs of the user. Creative writing and role playing scenarios can also help communication and cooperation across the team.

Scenarios are written in the third person narrative style and usually start by placing the persona in a specific context with a problem to solve. The story develops by describing how the interactive product delivers what the user requires in order to solve the problem and achieve the goal. In writing a scenario, it will start to become apparent what requirements are necessary for the interactive design to provide a good user experience. When used alongside personas and interpreted in UXD terms, simple scenarios like the one shown below can provide really useful pointers to a design team striving to provide a good user experience.

broad context

George and the Pre-Raphaelites

Last Thursday George's art teacher talked about the Pre-Raphaelites and mentioned that Manchester Art Gallery has a special collection of works by members of that movement.

Arriving home, George asked his parents if they could visit the gallery as this would be helpful to his studies and possibly a good day out.

specific focus

underlying motivation

George's mum needs more information before agreeing to organize a visit. She is keen to help George but needs to consider aspects of the trip including the timing, cost and travel arrangements. She accesses the museum's website with this task in mind and with the goal of making a decision on whether to make the trip or not. She knows that travelling to Manchester will take a least an hour ~o is interested to s~

defined needs

decision point

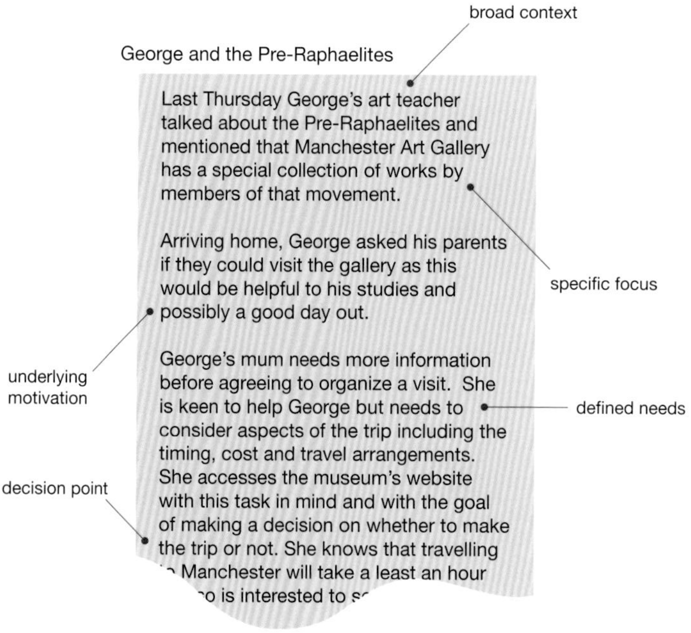

4.5
Meeting users' requirements
What do users hope to accomplish when they visit a website? Visitors to the webpage of Manchester Art Gallery may wish to check the opening times; preview the collections; find out about special exhibitions; or arrange an educational visit for a large group. All of these potential scenarios, and others, are catered for in the uncluttered layout and unambiguous navigation designed by Reading Room.

4.5

www.manchestergalleries.org ✕

▸ About Us ▸ Venue Hire ▸ Contact Us ▸ Our Other Venues ▸ Site Map   Search [   ] GO

Manchester Art Gallery

Shop online
Beautiful cards, prints and other items inspired by our exhibitions and the collection.

Text Size: A A A

| Home | Planning Your Visit | What's On | The Collections | Education | Families | Shop & Café | Supporting Us |

Thursday lates

Thursday lates

See art in a different light with a mix of live music, food and drink - late into the evening.

Free entry

Open Monday - Sunday
10am - 5pm

Late night opening on Thursday until 9pm
Closed 29 March 2013

Location
Mosley Street, Manchester
M2 3JL
Tel: 0161 235 8888

Gallery announcements

Keep in Touch

Venue Hire

Gallery of Costume

Twitter

Facebook

Please make a donation

creativetourist.com
Find out what Manchester has to offer for the creative tourist

Wonder Women: Radical Manchester
In April 1913 three ordinary Edwardian women turn vigilante, surprising guards at Manchester Art Gallery.

Events

Highlights tour
07 Mar 2013
▾ More

**Thursday Lates
Wonder : Women**
07 Mar 2013
▾ More

Mini Art Club
08 Mar 2013
▾ More

Mini Art Club
08 Mar 2013
▾ More

Channel Crossings ❯   Go to Events ❯

Planning Your Visit

New to the gallery, Using the gallery, Access, What's On, Shop and Cafe

What's On

Exhibitions, Events, Community Programmes, Permanent Galleries, Connected, Manchester's Museums and Galleries

Read reviews about Manchester Art Gallery on ⊚⊚ trip advisor.co.uk

The Collections

Search the collection, Highlights of the collection, About the collection, Collections in focus, Permanent Galleries, About the online collection, Recent acquisitions

Education

Plan Your Visit, Early Years, Primary KS1, Primary KS2, Secondary, Post 16 & HE/FE, Continuous professional development

YOUR PAINTINGS

Explore all of Manchester Art Gallery's oil paintings on the BBC's Your Paintings website.

Families

Visiting with your family, Clore Interactive Gallery, Events Calendar, Family art clubs

Shop & Cafe

Gallery Cafe, Shop Information, Picture Library

Supporting Us

Corporate Involvement, Schools Programme Sponsorship, Friends and Patrons, Get Involved, Creative Consultants

Volunteering

Why volunteer with us?, Volunteer opportunities, Volunteer experiences, More information about volunteering

Home | Planning Your Visit | What's On | The Collections | Education | Families | Shop & Cafe | Supporting Us
About Us | Venue Hire | Contact Us | Our Other Venues | Site Map | Accessibility | Copyright | Privacy/Disclaimer

A key benefit of taking a UXD approach is the amount of useful information that is available when specifying design requirements. Data from user research activities will help to define the scope of the project and to provide focus for the project team. Techniques applied to model users and their behaviour through personas and scenarios will provide insights into the context of use. This is beneficial because it centres the design plans on the needs of users from an early stage in the project, and places user experience at the forefront of everyone's thinking.

Where to start?

A good place to start the design process is by creating a list of initial design requirements. They are called 'initial' requirements because at the early stages of the process the team needs to take a flexible approach. A balance needs to be achieved between the requirement to provide a good user experience, the requirements of the client and the technical requirements of the systems on which the interaction will take place. In some situations it is necessary to knowingly degrade the user experience where there is a cost benefit in doing so.

A requirement that the user interface employs a clean visual design with no distractions is desirable from the user experience perspective. The need to add links and advertising information may be desirable from a commercial perspective, and there could be a technical solution that helps to reduce the negative impact on the user experience of a cluttered user interface. It is the job of the project team to recognize competing requirements and to use every tool at their disposal to achieve a balance.

Is there a better solution?

In any design process there can be a temptation to accept the first solution to a design problem. In our experience, students of design avoid looking for a better solution to a problem if an adequate solution seems to have been found. In an iterative design process, all ideas need to be challenged and evaluated after there has been an opportunity for them to be properly considered. If ideas are immediately challenged then it will prove difficult to get the project rolling. By allowing time between the development of ideas and the start of a cycle of design evaluation, a project will have a chance to take shape. After formulating a strong set of design ideas, the project becomes a candidate for participation in design development and testing by users and (in some cases) clients.

Specifying the requirements

Design requirements can be specified in relation to the user, product and system. In the case of the design of a digital video player one of many design requirements could say:

User: Michael likes to watch slow motion replays on TV and would use that feature when watching home-movies of his own children playing football.

Product: The user interface will have functions to instantly replay video at normal speed, half-speed or double speed.

System: The system needs to synthesize slow video using repeating frames.

Who specifies the requirements?

Team members will usually promote the needs of their particular area of expertise in the specification of requirements. It is essential to have a UXD project leader who can provide a balanced perspective on user research, user interface design and technical developments to mediate and move the project forward.

'The only way you can find a good answer is to clearly understand the question. You can't find the answer by using somebody else's answer to another question.'
– Saul Bass

Effective UXD project leaders are adept at encouraging excellent communication and morale in a project team. They unite researchers, visual designers, interaction designers, technologists and programmers behind a common goal of creating interactive products that users really love. A good team will learn from each other and create design solutions that could not be conceived or developed without a multi-talented joint effort.

Planning

It is beneficial to identify specific stages in a project and plan for them well in advance. The careful scheduling of people and resources is needed to keep a project on track because team members may be working on multiple projects at different stages. For this reason, it is a good idea to keep the team size as small as is practical and locate team members so that they can meet easily and regularly.

0	⌐ ▣	▼ Public Interest Law Institute		2/24/12	9/30/12	7.79 months	$410,910.00	
1	❶	▼ Rebrand & Website Redesign		2/24/12	9/30/12	7.79 months	$410,910.00	
2	❷	▼ Discovery		2/24/12	3/14/12	2.6 weeks	$27,850.00	
3		▷ Background Research		2/24/12	2/24/12	4 hours	$550.00	
8		▷ Stakeholder Round Table		2/24/12	2/27/12	1 day	$1,100.00	
13		▷ Stakeholder Interviews	8	2/27/12	3/5/12	1 week	$7,000.00	
18		▷ Expert Evaluation	8	2/27/12	3/5/12	1 week	$6,200.00	
24		▷ User Interviews	8	2/27/12	3/12/12	2 weeks	$7,600.00	ID; PM; C.D.
29		▷ Requirements Prioritization	24	3/12/12	3/14/12	2 days	$5,400.00	E.D.D.; PM; C.S.; C.I
35		▼ Rebranding	24	3/12/12	6/1/12	2.95 months	$174,460.00	
36		▼ Brand Name		3/12/12	3/27/12	2.2 weeks	$15,980.00	
37		▷ Stakeholder Round Table		3/12/12	3/13/12	1 day	$1,340.00	D.; PM; C.D.; M.S.;
43		▷ Design Round 1	37	3/13/12	3/20/12	1 week	$7,320.00	
49		▷ Design Round 2	43	3/20/12	3/27/12	1 week	$7,320.00	sign Round 2 ☐
55		▼ Messaging Strategy	37	3/13/12	3/30/12	2.6 weeks	$26,280.00	
56		▷ Design Round 1		3/13/12	3/20/12	1 week	$10,680.00	
62		▷ Design Round 2	56	3/20/12	3/27/12	1 week	$8,600.00	sign Round 2 ☐
68		▷ Style Guide	62	3/27/12	3/30/12	3 days	$7,000.00	
74		▼ Visual Identity	36	3/27/12	4/23/12	3.8 weeks	$46,720.00	
75		▷ Visual Design Round 1		3/27/12	4/5/12	1.4 weeks	$18,760.00	Visu
82		▷ Visual Design Round 2	75	4/5/12	4/16/12	1.4 weeks	$17,520.00	
88		▷ Style Guide	82	4/16/12	4/23/12	1 week	$10,440.00	
93		▼ Collateral & Other Print Materials	88	4/23/12	6/1/12	1.45 months	$85,480.00	
94		▷ Visual Design Round 1 & 2	82	4/23/12	5/28/12	1.25 months	$78,560.00	
101		▷ Pre–Press Check	94	5/28/12	6/1/12	4 days	$6,920.00	
106		▼ Website Redesign	68	3/30/12	7/13/12	3.75 months	$208,600.00	
107		▼ Content		3/30/12	4/24/12	3.4 weeks	$30,760.00	
108		▷ Content Audit & Strategy		3/30/12	4/17/12	2.4 weeks	$24,400.00	
114		▷ Style Guide	108	4/17/12	4/24/12	1 week	$6,360.00	
120		▼ Information Architecture	107	4/24/12	5/29/12	1.25 months	$63,000.00	
121		▷ Wireframe Round 1		4/24/12	5/8/12	2 weeks	$28,400.00	

Project planning is an art requiring foresight and the ability to think along parallel timelines. Some tasks in the UXD process can be undertaken at the same time or overlap other tasks. User research, stakeholder analysis and user modelling activities can overlap in most projects. It is a good idea to identify tasks that could hold up the project if they are not completed on time. For example, wireframes that visualize the underlying structure of an interface need to incorporate the functional elements of the design. This means that wireframe creation is an activity dependent on the functional specification being ready.

Aids to planning

Computer-based tools designed to make it easier to schedule tasks, match resources to tasks and identify task dependencies include Microsoft Project and Merlin. Some really good web-based tools that offer team collaboration and file management features in addition to project scheduling are Basecamp (basecamp.com) and Zoho (zoho.com). Both Basecamp and Zoho offer free versions for smaller projects.

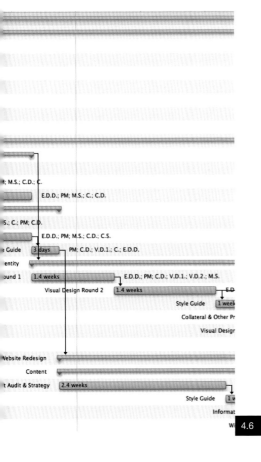

4.6
An aid to planning
Merlin was used to produce this Gantt chart and to manage the budget for a print and web design project. In the table on the left each task and subtask is identified, scheduled and budgeted. The visualization on the right contains a timeline for each task making it easy to see the sequence of tasks, which tasks can be done at the same time (in parallel) and those that need to be done sequentially because they depend on preceding tasks being completed (shown by lines and arrows).

Garry Byrne, Managing Director and owner of Powered by Reason

Garry Byrne is head of Powered by Reason, a Manchester-based (UK) strategic, creative and technical digital agency. Garry explains how the design planning for a digital project has evolved from a client-initiated, product-focused approach to a more iterative approach that considers the user and the context at different stages.

How it was

Not long ago, most projects could be delivered using a very simple process. It started with a chat with the client, so you could find out what they want. Next, you went away and did a bit of thinking, coming up with a design that would fulfil those client needs. After that, you'd agree, in the form of a specification and maybe some prototypes, exactly what it is you are going to deliver to the client. Finally, you'd go away and actually build the 'thing': something that looks pretty and delivers on the agreed requirements. Say, a great-looking website which allowed your clients to sell their custom t-shirt designs online (see figure 4.7).

4.7

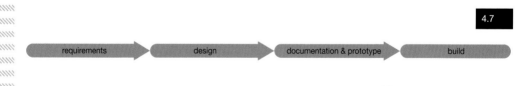

requirements → design → documentation & prototype → build

4.7
A linear design model
Find out what the client wants; come up with a design; specify what it will do; and then build it. This approach may appeal to the client, as they will understand it, but it may not result in the best outcome for them or the user.

How it changed

Projects can still be delivered this way, but it is not really robust enough for modern digital development. It still has a place in the sales process, however: with 30 minutes or so allocated for you to pitch your company to the client, you can't hang around explaining the myriad angles your approach will take in order to get to the right conclusion. For that reason, a linear process is usually the one we describe when talking to clients at the sales stage.

Over the years, the design planning process evolved to allow a more iterative, research-led approach. All of a sudden, your design requirements can influence user requirements, and you can re-visit your agreed specification as you get through the project, as you have the opportunity to test actual 'stuff' with actual users.

In truth, all that really happened was that we added a few arrow heads to the workflow diagram (see figure 4.8).

How it should be

For a while, this was adequate, but simply adding iteration to an otherwise linear process is no longer sufficient in a world where trends come and go, often before most people have heard about them. 'Social' is no longer just adding a Facebook 'like' button and a Twitter feed, and even the most mature and preconceived online task can be improved through careful consideration, research and planning as part of the process.

Your target audience is less patient, less loyal and more eager to get involved than ever before; to speak to them effectively, your process needs to make sure that you've considered everything. The goal is simplicity, and behind the simplest idea we'll need a stack of planning and analysis to work out the complexities and remove them from the final result.

4.8

```
requirements  →  ←  design  →  ←  documentation & prototype  →  ←  build
```

4.8
Changing the linear process
A slightly more iterative design model: all the same activities as in the linear approach above, but the stages are allowed to feed into each other.

To better describe a modern digital project process, we firstly need to remove what is probably the biggest flaw in the traditional project process: the linearity. Whilst you undoubtedly need a deliverable at some point, to represent this in a linear format is to constrain yourself to the idea that a deliverable is an end point.

Modern projects are organic, adaptive beasts, and your process needs to reflect this: You need to be able to consider user requirements not just at project initiation, but right through design, documentation and development. Your initial research and planning activities should be just the start of an ongoing effort to learn and improve; there should be no reason why you can't go back to your clients after your prototype stage and suggest radical changes or additions to the project, rather than simply trying to 'rubberstamp' the work done so far.

In addition, a modern project process will take into account social media requirements, user testing and technical planning, even if they are not a fundamental part of your agreement.

Most importantly, your final deliverable needs to stop being 'final'. It is practically impossible to deliver the perfect digital project nowadays, and while it is still early days in terms of our clients realizing that they need to commit to post-launch testing and iteration, we can at least make sure our process is built to accommodate it in readiness (see figure 4.9).

4.9

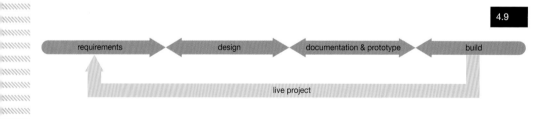

4.9
The iterative approach
A cyclical design process model that reflects the iterative nature of modern digital projects.

The iterative approach

Whilst still simplistic, the cyclical model shown in figure 4.9 gives a feel for the iterative nature of modern project delivery: plan; design; prototype; build; launch; repeat. The 'launch' is no longer a final output, and becomes part of an organic journey of discovery and improvement (see figure 4.10).

But if we really want to represent the true journey to modern project planning, we need to recognize the complex nature of defining the requirements for the project. This involves learning about who the users are, and translating this into useful personas; identifying emerging trends and habits to provide extra value to our users; and recognizing the wider business strategy, timescale and budget of the client.

4.10

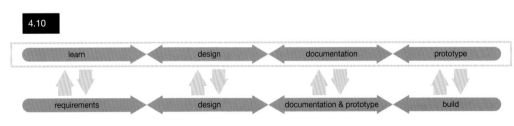

4.10
The iterative process
A modern design model which identifies the complexities of the users and clients' requirements as part of the iterative process.

Reviewing the process

Every time we go through the cycle, we need to consider every aspect of planning, research and impact: What can we do with the time and budget we have? Is the business capable of actually responding to the social interest we would generate? Who are we targeting and why? Does this support, align with, or contradict other business activity?

This process takes longer, but if you are looking for something that will not only bring you better results, but will also make your life easier in the long run, then it is an approach you need to be applying to every project you undertake.

Of course, our clients are not yet ready to launch their next website in an iterative format; they're still looking for a finite delivery produced on a fixed price basis. But we have to communicate to them that the beauty of a cyclical process is one of scale: it can be applied to a whole project, or just to individual elements of a project as required. We can do this by synthesizing the comfort of a linear approach with the cycles of the iterative approach (see figure 4.11).

4.11

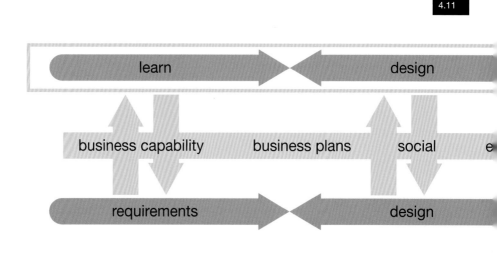

learn   design

business capability   business plans   social   e

requirements   design

The best of both worlds

This way, we have the linear process that allows us to present an end point to the client (and deal with the fixed budget and time frames our clients tend to love), yet ensures that we are thinking about everything at every point in the process.

It is not enough to simply iterate any more – increasingly, project success will be defined by the amount of planning and research that happened at every stage, rather than the ability to tweak a design by changing colours based on user feedback.

4.11
Linear or iterative – both
The final design planning process provides the client with a straight-forward sequence that works towards a tangible product, but allows multiple opportunities to test, re-specify and re-build, using the various tools for research, prototyping and analysis that are available to the UX designer.

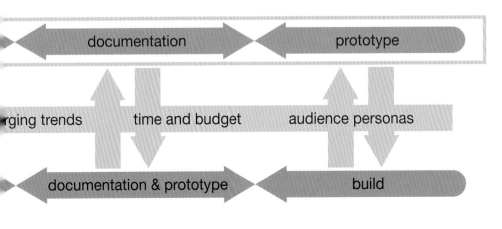

documentation · prototype

rging trends · time and budget · audience personas

documentation & prototype · build

For a designer, working to standards is sometimes seen as a burden rather than a benefit, particularly when doing so requires design compromises. In the early days of web design, accessibility requirements for websites were seldom considered by designers of visually rich sites. Where accessibility was considered, the technology in use often required users to revert to text-only pages. In 1999 the Web Content Accessibility Guidelines (WCAG) were published by the World Wide Web Consortium and this, together with updated HTML and pressure from disability groups, forced a change in thinking by designers and developers. When sites were redesigned to be accessible, it was often found that the changes improved the user experience for everyone – not just for those with sight loss, hearing loss, mobility or cognitive impairments.

From the designer's point of view, working to standards provides another way to show evidence of professional competence. Standards are regularly updated and so help to ensure that working practices are up-to-date and that designers apply the latest thinking in design and technology.

In UXD, there are two standards bodies that have particular significance and, as in the case of web accessibility, have the influence to affect many aspects of interactive design.

1. The World Wide Web Consortium (W3C) (w3.org) is an international community where member organizations, a full-time staff and the public work together to develop web standards. Led by web inventor Tim Berners-Lee and CEO Jeffrey Jaffe, W3C's mission is to lead the Web to its full potential.

2. ISO (International Organization for Standardization) (iso.org) is the world's largest developer of voluntary international standards. International standards give state-of-the-art specifications for products, services and good practice, helping to make industry more efficient and effective. Developed through global consensus, they help to break down barriers to international trade.

4.12
Use of ISO
This diagram is adapted from one within the ISO 9241-210 document. It shows that user-centred design does not follow a strict linear process and illustrates that each human-centred design activity uses outputs from other activities. Design activities continue in an iterative cycle until the solution meets the requirements.

At the time of writing, the international standard most relevant to UXD is Part 210 of ISO 9241: Human-centred design for interactive systems. It is called Part 210 because it forms just one part of a group of standards within the Ergonomics of Human–System Interaction. Other areas include Part 11: Guidance on usability, and Part 920: Guidance on tactile and haptic interactions.

Part 210 describes six principles of user-centred design and provides guidance on how to apply them:

➜ The design is based upon an explicit understanding of users, tasks and environments.

➜ Users are involved throughout design and development.

➜ The design is driven and refined by user-centred evaluation.

➜ The process is iterative.

➜ The design addresses the whole user experience.

➜ The design team includes multidisciplinary skills and perspectives.

4.12

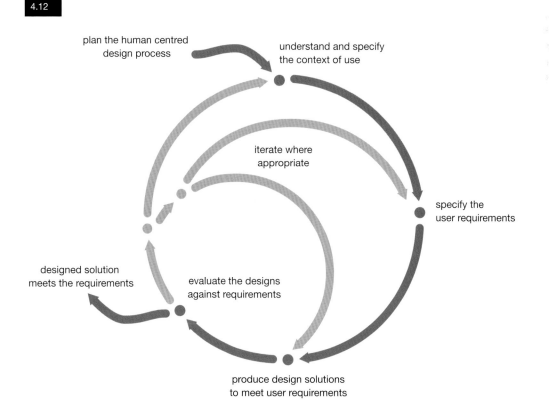

plan the human centred design process

understand and specify the context of use

iterate where appropriate

specify the user requirements

designed solution meets the requirements

evaluate the designs against requirements

produce design solutions to meet user requirements

In this activity, you will construct a solution to a simplified interactive design project. The solution will take the form of an outline plan that can include a few rough sketches. The plan aims to describe a practical solution that satisfies the requirements of the design. It will explain the sequence of tasks that the user will need to complete in a path towards achieving their goals. The objective is to keep the burden of tasks to the minimum necessary to achieve the goals while also providing a good user experience.

A scenario that identifies a user context is provided, although this can be changed if required. The activity in Chapter 5 will take the result of this solution forward to the prototyping stage.

Activity (allow 2–3 hours)

Step 1
Read through the following problem and think about how the user will begin the interaction. Try to develop empathy with the user and think through their situation and the challenges they face. How can your design solution communicate a shared understanding of the problem, instil confidence and function effectively? You are recommended to use pencil and paper for this activity. Sticky notes and an eraser will help.

Problem and context:

A university student in their final year needs to find information on opportunities for progression into employment or further study. User research has been conducted and user goals have been identified:

➔ to be aware of all relevant opportunities as they arise;

➔ to have sufficient information to make informed choices;

➔ to reduce the time spent filtering non-relevant opportunities;

➔ to save and recall specific information to allow later review;

➔ to share specific information with others when required.

In response to the user goals the design team have specified the following requirements:

➔ a smartphone application with access to extensive and relevant data sources;

➔ functions that filter the data depending on the user's requirements;

➔ functions that intelligently highlight new and interesting opportunities as they arise;

➔ functions to save and recall data;

➔ functions to share data.

Step 2

Interaction framework and platform:

In Step 3 you are going to need to explain how the user starts interacting with the design. Before you can do this, it is necessary to understand the interaction framework offered by the platform – in this case a smartphone application. If you are not familiar with smartphone applications then take some time to investigate the types of interaction available and the characteristic features of the smartphone platform. These generally include touch screen, haptic (tactile) feedback, geolocation, motion detection, and camera and audio functions for recording and playback.

An interactive application is made up of functional elements and informational elements. Functional elements need to be recognized by the user as controls or as part of the framework of an application. Informational elements, such as images and text, need to be recognized as passive content that may change but do not work as controls. There can be crossover between functional and passive elements. In some situations, an image can also be a control (e.g. to enlarge itself when clicked) and text can also be a control (e.g. acting as a navigation link). Before starting to build the solution make a list of the elements you expect to see in the application and identify them either as functional or informational. Keep an eye on where these elements are used and review their status as functional or informational. Think how the user will understand what type of element they are by the context in which they are found and their appearance.

Activity 4
Exploring solutions

Step 3

Define the entry point and the interaction options that you are providing for the user. Write down what the user can see and what the user can do. It will help to draw simple boxes representing the interface elements. Identify how the user goals are brought closer for the user by following each of the interaction options you have defined. From this point forward, you are constructing the solution and creating the experience. If any of the interactions do not advance the user forward to one or more of their goals then consider changing or removing it.

Step 4

For every possible user interaction option (created in Step 3) make a connection to the result of choosing that option. Repeat the process outlined in Step 3, taking the user further along the path toward achieving their goals. Continue until you have created a solution that achieves all of the user goals.

Step 5

Invent a few individual user scenarios like the ones below to test your solution and see how it performs.

'Dave is sitting in a cafe with a friend from his course. At the end of their current courses they both want to progress to a relevant postgraduate course in the USA. They each study different subjects but want to stay within a four-hour drive of each other so that they can meet up at weekends.'

'Gemma is a student graphic designer and wants to find a graduate-level job in London. She is aware that any opportunities are quickly snapped up and wants to be alerted to new ones as they arise so that she has the best chance of making a successful application.'

Tip

Have you considered that new users of the application may need a different entry point to existing users? What sort of information may the user want to see before continuing with their interaction?

Step 6

Review your solution and improve it until you are confident that it works reasonably well for the individual user scenarios that you have invented. The next stage is to make it accessible for others to test. To do this, you will need to convert your notes and sketches into something that a user can recognize and interact with. The activity in Chapter 5 is designed to help you do this.

Conclusion

If this is your first attempt at designing an interactive application then this activity is likely to have been revealing and probably quite difficult. We hope that you were slightly frustrated by the minimal information provided in the problem statement in Step 1, the lack of detail about the interaction framework in Step 2, and the difficulty of achieving what users want in Step 5. If you think that you need to go back, improve the user research and define the problem more closely before starting to develop solutions, then that is probably true. If you think that you have a better understanding of the problem by attempting to solve it, then that seems likely too.

The exercise has been successful if you recognize the need to start exploring solutions early in a project's development and see that user research is key to defining the shape of the project solution.

Tip

Is the user able to form a logical mental model o§ndo a simple mistake such as choosing the wrong option or mistyping something?

Design methods

Here, we offer a UXD perspective on interactive design methods in practice. The development of new digital platforms and technologies makes it an exciting and inventive process. The technology exists to locate the position of anything on the planet, augment reality by superimposing digital environments on the real world, and converse with intelligent computers who speak just like we do.

As new technologies arrive, so do opportunities to improve the user experience. Sometimes, though, in the scramble to be first with new features, the user experience can be degraded. To avoid this, the UXD team needs to remain focused on the user's requirements and to apply design methods that achieve the best user experience.

A digital media platform is a system that users recognize as a distinct way to interact with digital media applications. The platform can often be independent of the hardware device. Facebook have worked hard to develop their original website into a social media platform that can be accessed on the Web through smartphone apps and through other devices such as smart TVs. Users recognize Facebook as a place to communicate and share different types of media. Designers adapt the Facebook interface to provide a similar experience to users across a range of different devices. Users modify their expectations of what they can do with Facebook when using devices with different capabilities, screen sizes and input methods.

5.1
Adding value
New technologies such as augmented reality (AR) have the power to add extra value to all types of experiences. Arart is a stunning example of how these new technologies can enhance familiar and enjoyable pastimes such as reading an illustrated book, visiting famous works of art in a gallery, or studying the sleeve notes of your favourite album. The software recognizes underlying images displayed by the camera in hand-held devices. The application then brings these to life with inventive animations (arart.info).

The web as a platform

The Web is an open platform that can support a wide range of technologies and devices. Complex websites accessed through a browser can be developed to the level of a platform. Huge sites such as Facebook, eBay and Amazon all fall into this category. When responding to a client brief to provide a new website, it is a good idea to consider the limitations of an isolated website approach. A project may be more successful from a UXD perspective if delivered as a web application within an existing platform, such as Facebook, or as a mobile application that can work on a range of devices and the Web.

Applications built on existing platforms provide benefits for the user, including authentication (no need to log-in), a familiar interface, opportunities for shared experiences, and access to services provided by the platform, such as user registration and geolocation data. Benefits for the client include access to large numbers of potential users, built-in payment systems and opportunities to market their business through social media.

When embarking on a design project, the objective is to produce the required outcomes for clients, users and stakeholders. This rather obvious statement hides an uncomfortable fact that design teams can sometimes lose sight of the required outcomes. Instead, they may focus on meeting requirements that have crept into the design process since the required outcomes were identified through user research. The team needs to be clear about what it is they are designing, what the user requirements are, and what functionality needs to be created in order to fulfil the user requirements. Beyond this, they also need to consider client, stakeholder and technical requirements.

5.2
All Star Lanes
If you have already decided to go bowling tonight, you probably have very specific requirements: find the venue; book the lane; tell your friends. You probably do not need a hard sell about the pleasures that bowling has to offer. All Star Lanes has a number of boutique bowling alleys across the UK. Their Maek-designed website is a visually seductive experience on a personal computer or tablet, but adapts to different devices, foregrounding the information and tools that are likely to be required by a user on the move.

Requirements statements

Once the desired outcomes of an interactive design are understood, it is useful to define the requirements in 'requirements statements'. These documents will typically be managed by the UXD project leader and become the focus for those with responsibility for creating the design and achieving the functionality. They also serve to inform the client about what the project aims to deliver within the agreed budget.

A 'requirements statement' will usually have a hierarchical structure, with essential requirements at the top of the hierarchy and supporting requirements lower down. Because the design process is iterative, it is very likely that the statements will need to be revised during the development stage of the project. The possibility of this happening can be reduced by:

➔ maintaining a clear focus on the user experience rather than on developing features;

➔ applying the best design approaches to achieve the required functionality;

➔ linking and simplifying different requirements, e.g. creating a responsive design rather than multiple designs.

5.2

An experience can be thought of as a journey during which we will interact with different types of digital information. For example, a user may retrieve a catalogue entry for a product, upload and collate some photos, watch a video, write a review, or edit a wiki article; and each subsequent encounter adds to the residue of digital data. Each artefact in this mass of data is a unique resource with the potential to shape the user experience, but this will happen only when the information is arranged in a meaningful way.

The purpose of semantic design is to devise a data-model, or information architecture (IA), for organizing information in a way that makes sense to people. When applied to designed experiences, semantics describe the way in which information is organized and interconnected in a meaningful way.

The purpose of semantic design is to devise a data-model (or Information architecture) for organizing information in a way that makes sense to people. It also defines the language (or syntax) for the systems that will store, link, exchange and interpret the data in order to personalize our experiences.

More and more experiences are going to be powered by this data. Users will need to find, retrieve, aggregate, create, edit and contextualize information with ease, and the experience will need to be researched and designed with this in mind.

Metadata means 'data about data', and it is embedded into digital documents: file names, properties and ownership are all types of metadata. In social media settings, we can often tag our information with pertinent metadata in order to contextualize it for a wider audience or to label it for future reference. Metadata is one of the means by which we can organize information in a way that makes sense to us.

5.3

5.3
A timeline for social media
Timeless by Justin Chen is a
concept for managing social
media. The platform uses the
principle of user-defined events
organized into a scrollable
timeline. Users can associate
media with each event in order
to provide an intuitive system for
curating personal collections of
memories.

Interactive design requires an understanding of design and development methods across a range of disciplines including graphic design, programming and user interface design. Professionals working in these areas often have years of experience using cherished tools and techniques to produce high-quality designs.

A visual designer or programmer taking a UXD project leader role will already have skills that can benefit the UXD process. The ability to sketch and draw aids communication with users and the team; the ability to collect and analyse data can help understand user trends. In addition to design and production skills, a UXD approach introduces the need for new tools and techniques to be mastered. Practical research, analysis and communication skills together with a particular mindset that recognizes the needs of users will require practice and experience to get right.

Empathy

Putting yourself in someone else's shoes is an expression used to help us comprehend the idea of empathy – the ability to understand what another person is feeling from their perspective. For some people being empathic is a part of their character, for others it is invisible and the experience of others will require regular explanation. Being empathic is part of the UXD mindset and it can be developed through the use of tools and techniques. The creation of scenarios and personas (see page 114–119) will help the design team to develop empathy because they are techniques that require a wider understanding of the target user group. Bringing users together with designers and developers early on in the project will also help to foster an empathic response to their situation.

➜ Empathy tools can be used to simulate barriers that may exist for a particular group of users. When designing for users with special conditions or disabilities, designers can wear devices that simulate the user's experience. Putting on a pair of weighted shoes can help designers understand the situation of people with mobility problems. When designing for people with impaired vision, wearing a pair of cloudy spectacles can help designers discover how well their designs work for that particular group of users.

➜ Personas can be empathic; describing what a user may feel in certain situations.

Communication and organization

Good communication is often cited as the hardest thing to achieve in team working and it can take effort by the project leader to encourage everyone to discuss and embrace the challenges of experience design. Members of the team need fluid communication channels, where they can share expertise, put forward ideas, work collaboratively and post status updates. Face-to-face meetings are important but need to be structured and managed so that they are also positive and productive. It may be necessary to support other members of the team in developing their communication and interpersonal skills, particularly if they are unfamiliar with a UXD approach. The project leader needs to be good at listening and able to recognize the importance of what it is being said, to moderate discussions and to help maintain a balance between competing interests.

'Empathy is defined as the ability to understand and share the feelings of another. But it's not enough to understand, we have to act. [...] Only when it is observable and experienced by others does it have impact.'
– Whitney Hess

➜ Project management tools can help a group to manage multiple projects. Code Computerlove use Redmine (redmine.org), which offers facilities to chart a project's progress, post documents and manage files. It can also track time spent on activities as well as technical issues in software development.

➜ Scrum is a tightly structured 'agile' software development framework that includes daily team-based decision making and prioritization of activities. There are a wide range of software tools and web applications that specifically support a Scrum framework, including Scrumy (scrumy.com/about).

➜ A range of project management tools are available as cloud-based web applications, each with slightly different features and support. One of the longest established and popular is Basecamp (basecamp.com).

➜ Project schedules are traditionally managed using Gantt charts that show project activities as a number of parallel timelines identifying resource use and duration. Each timeline can include events such as start dates, end dates and milestones in the development of a project. Tom's Planner (tomsplanner.com) is a popular web-based Gantt chart tool.

5.4

5.4
Capturing ideas
Pencil sketching is a really effective way to quickly externalize ideas. Sketches on paper can be captured using a digital camera or scanner, edited, stored and shared online.

5.5
Alternative to paper
A number of tablet devices offer a similar experience to sketching on paper using a stylus or finger drawing. These have the advantage that no paper is needed and sketches are originated in digital form, being editable and instantly available to share.

5.6
Keep it neat!
This stainless steel template helps the user to create neat and consistent user interface sketches. (Photo: William Sjahrial)

Ideation and problem solving

In every creative field it is necessary to capture good ideas and realize their potential. A good idea in your mind needs to be externalized quickly because you may otherwise forget it. If you externalize a fragment of an idea then that can be used as a starting point for a more developed idea at another time. There are many tools to assist in generating, externalizing and organizing ideas. In our experience the best ones keep things simple.

➔ A large whiteboard is a good tool to record ideas generated by groups. Smart whiteboards (smarttech.com) can be used in conjunction with a computer to record and replay sketches and notes. Flip-charts are good for recording and sequencing ideas that have been generated in group meetings. Individual sheets can be torn out of flip-charts and easily reorganized, passed around a group and edited.

➔ Sketch notes (sketchnotearmy.com) are a graphic approach to note taking and help to create a flow and draw links between different ideas. If there is someone in your team who has the ability to express ideas and concepts in sketch form then encourage them to create illustrated meeting notes.

➔ A quick way to capture ideas that occur in situations where it is difficult to take written notes is to use a smartphone to record audio or video. Files can be uploaded using a cloud-based file storage service and easily accessed from a desktop computer. Even a very basic mobile phone can be used to leave voice messages on your own message service for later retrieval. Evernote is the Swiss army knife of digital note taking (evernote.com).

➔ Gamestorming and brainstorming are structured activities designed to heighten ideation and problem solving in groups. A moderator is designated to lead a group in goal-orientated activities which may include role play, improvization and the random association of different ideas. There are some really good examples made available at the Gamestorming website (gogamestorm.com)

5.7
Hierarchies and navigation
Putting coloured sticky notes on a wall is a simple way of exploring content hierarchies and navigation. Simply write a different topic or content description on each note and arrange them on a wall. The position of each note will define its place in the structure of the interactive design. Notes can be connected by strips of paper, arranged in functional groups, placed in a hierarchy depending on their position and may use colour to identify a particular attribute. Users and stakeholders may discover how they would expect to navigate the structure of a proposed interactive design.

Maps and flows

Tools that help visualize the flow of an interactive system allow a team to develop and refine the underlying architecture. Diagrams and charts offer a good way to analyse interaction scenarios and remove potential problems at an early stage. Some tools make it possible to automatically map existing websites by following all possible navigation options and displaying them in a linked hierarchical chart.

➔ Flowcharts and diagrams can be hand-drawn or created using software tools such as Creatley (creately.com) or Microsoft Visio.

➔ Storyboards are traditionally used in linear film-making where they are used to visualize a script in a sequence of hand-drawn scenes. They are also used in interactive design as a quick way to visualize an interface and describe a typical sequence of events in its use. Printable templates for storyboarding are available online or can be easily created. Presentation software such as Powerpoint or Keynote can be used for storyboarding and also provide options for easily sequencing storyboard frames in a non-linear way.

5.7

Working with users

Conducting user research is potentially the most time consuming and costly aspect of a UXD approach. Any tool or technique that can help you get a better understanding of your users is better than none, particularly if the results are reasonably accurate and the cost is low. Time spent with users can be supervised, for example in face-to-face meetings and workshops, or unsupervised, such as when users respond to an online survey or provide feedback on a prototype that is accessed online. Supervised time is generally referred to as moderated and unsupervised activities are termed un-moderated.

➜ Before recruiting a pool of users to engage in initial research that is specific to your project, consider what can be achieved through desk research and data gathering. Organizations such as the UK Design Council undertake ethnographic research into particular topics and the results of these are made available to designers (designcouncil.org.uk).

➜ Card sorting is a user activity that can deliver insights into what users expect from an interactive design. The elements of the design are described on individual cards and the user is asked to arrange them into a logical structure. Card sorting can be moderated or un-moderated with sessions delivered face-to-face or online. Optimal Workshop offers an online tool for running remote card sorting sessions (optimalworkshop.com).

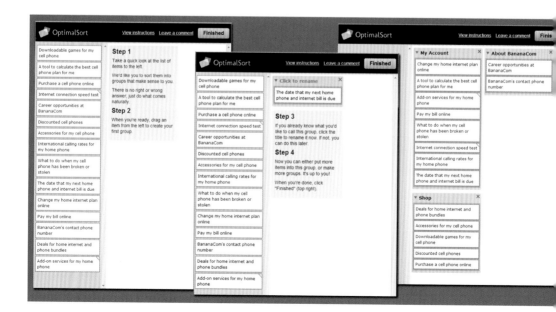

➜ Contextual inquiry is a tool of user research that aims to provide a realistic view of users and their environment. It involves spending time with users and observing their activities in the context of the proposed interactive design. This could be at home or at work or in a specific situation, such as using a public transport ticketing system. A well-designed contextual inquiry will reveal aspects of the user experience that will be missed by other forms of research, but it is expensive to undertake. A good primer to conducting a contextual inquiry, written by Pooja Chinnapattan, can be found at Webcredible (webcredible.co.uk).

➜ A content experiment is a way to test different versions of a live website. The design team can receive minute-by-minute reports of their success in delivering goals for the user and for the site owners. The method is a development of A-B testing where two versions of a web page are compared by alternating their availability to users. Content experiments allow discreet changes to a web page's content to be made and tested. Content experiments make it possible to measure the reaction of users to different visual and interaction elements and refine designs in an objective and quantifiable way. Google leads the way in website analytics and content experiments (google.com/analytics/features/content.html).

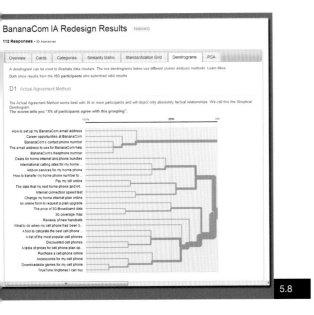

5.8

5.8
Card sorting tool
OptimalSort is a web-based card sorting tool from Optimal Workshop. In this example participants are asked to group the information and functions offered by a telecom company's website. Users can drag cards (the statements on the left) into a blank space on the right to create and name a new collection. Users drag more cards into a collection, create more collections and move cards between collections to visualize their idea of the site's information architecture. When the user has finished sorting all the cards the data is submitted and analysed with tests from other users. Optimal Workshop provide a range of visualizations of the data including the dendrogram shown on the right.

Prototyping

A prototype (or mock-up) is a model of an interactive design that can be used as a basis for developing improvements in the design. A prototype can be low fidelity, meaning that it looks and feels like a sketchbook version of the design; or it can be high fidelity, meaning that it simulates the look and feel of the proposed final design. Prototypes should be created as early as possible in a project's development. They should be tested thoroughly to provide confidence in the things that do work and reveal the things that don't work. Initial versions are best created in low fidelity so that clients, users and the design team recognize that they represent a work in progress and realize that they are free to suggest ways to make improvements. Some members of the design team may argue that it is easier to make a functional and finished design than create a prototype. They are missing the point of prototyping and probably need to improve their skills in quickly creating effective mock-ups.

➜ Wireframes are visual prototypes that reveal the underlying structure of interactive designs as a grid. There are many tools for creating wireframes, including Pencil which is free, works on all platforms and is open-source (pencil.evolus.vn).

➜ Interactive prototypes take the mock-up a step further by simulating an interactive session, allowing a user to navigate through the design. Sophisticated tools such as Microsoft Sketchflow (microsoft.com/silverlight/ sketchflow/) allows prototypes to be tested online and contextual notes added for the design team to review. High-fidelity prototypes need high quality interface graphics to appear real to the user. More realism can be achieved by delivering an interactive prototype on the platform for which the design is intended.

5.9–5.10
Presenting and amending protoypes
Interactive HTML website wireframes or high-fidelity mock-ups can be produced without coding using Axure prototyping software. A link to the prototype can be sent to clients or users to evaluate the design, on smartphones or on the Web. Changes to designs can be made much more easily because the functionality is simulated, requiring no production-stage coding or resources (azure.com).

5.9

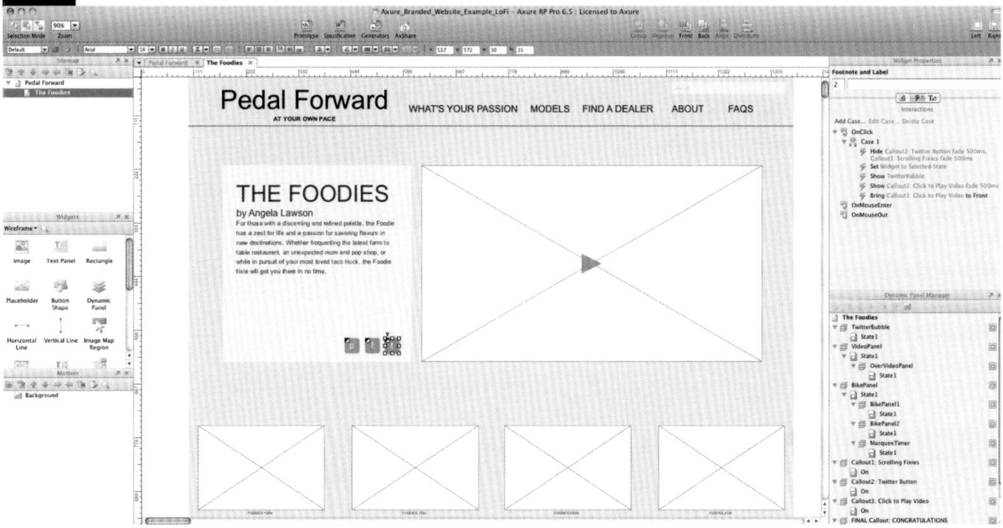
Axure_Branded_Website_Example_LoFi - Axure RP Pro 6.5 : Licensed to Axure
Pedal Forward
AT YOUR OWN PACE
WHAT'S YOUR PASSION
MODELS
FIND A DEALER
ABOUT
FAQS
THE FOODIES
by Angela Lawson
For those with a discerning and refined palette, the Foodie has a zest for life and a passion for savoring flavors in new destinations. Whether frequenting the latest farm to table restaurant, an unexpected mom and pop shop, or while in pursuit of your most loved taco truck, the Foodie fixie will get you there in no time.

5.10

Axure_Branded_Website_Example - Axure RP Pro 6.5 : Licensed to Axure
Pedal Forward
AT YOUR OWN PACE
WHAT'S YOUR PASSION?
MODELS
FIND A DEALER
ABOUT
FAQS
THE FOODIES
by Angela Lawson
For those with a discerning and refined palette, the Foodie has a zest for life and a passion for savoring flavors in new destinations. Whether frequenting the latest farm to table restaurant, an unexpected mom and pop shop, or while in pursuit of your most loved taco truck, the Foodie fixie will get you there in no time.
Me, my food and my bike...

In some situations, users will enjoy an innovative and unusual interface. They will delight in the process of exploring and discovering what they need to do to interact and navigate through the content. Along the way they will learn the language and controls of the interface and unconsciously commit this knowledge to memory. When they return they will know what to do without the need to explore.

Creating and customizing

The human capacity to recall an interface design can offer designers a shortcut to creating new interactive designs that are already familiar to users. Design patterns are reusable templates that include elements of structure and control that users recognize. They can be customized or 'skinned' to match specific design requirements while keeping the use pattern intact. This has advantages, particularly in common user interface situations such as file management, and navigating through options and operating peripherals such as a camera or printer. Design patterns often exist as just an image collection of different visual interfaces. They can also exist as software libraries that include the functional as well as the visual pattern. Interactive designs created as applications will often incorporate interface elements provided within the development environment. This is why user controls to select a date or choose a value from a list appear identical in many applications on the Apple iPhone but are handled differently on Google Android and other smartphone systems.

Problems with design patterns

The use of appropriate design patterns can be helpful to the user experience but there are some pitfalls to avoid. If the design pattern uses custom labels or icons that are unfamiliar to the user then they will need to learn what they mean and what they do. A Sony PlayStation controller includes symbols that are abstract and require the user to develop an association between the symbol and the function it controls. In some cases the function changes with the context of the interaction. Designers need to provide support for first-time users of interactive applications so that abstract or hidden controls can be discovered and learned.

Other problems can be caused for the user if the use pattern is modified. When the user subconsciously recognizes a design pattern and expects it to behave in a certain way – then it should.

5.11
Patternry Open
Patternry Open is a library of user interface patterns offering examples, guidance on usage and, in some cases, example code.

5.11

← → www.patternry.com ✕

Front Page **Patterns** Tour Plans & Pricing About Pattern Ideas Give Feedback Blog

🐦 Follow us   📘 Like   402

Patternry

Sign In | Sign Up

Main   Tags ▾

Search in patterns

Patternry Open

Patternry Open is a free front-end resource for anyone who wants to design and develop great Websites or applications. You can build a similar resource for yourself or your company with Patternry.

View: **All Patterns (43)** | Full (30) | Mini (7) HTML (6)

Sort by: **Date** | Alphabetical

HORIZONTAL MODULE TABS

WUFOO

▼ Add a Field   ▶ Field Settings   ▶ Form

Standard

ABC Single Line Text   123 Number

¶ Paragraph Text   ☑ Checkbox

DRAG AND DROP MODULES

ACCORDION   html

Collapsible Group Red

Red is the color of blood, a ruby, and strawberries. I visible spectrum of light, and is commonly associate beauty, blood, anger, socialism and communism, an happiness.

Collapsible Group Violet

Collapsible Group Orange

NAVIGATION LIST   html

LIST HEADER

Home

Library

Applications

ANOTHER LIST HEADER

Settings

MULTICON-PAGE PAGINATION   html

| « | 1 | 2 | 3 | 4 | » |

| « | 10 | 11 | 12 | » |

| ← | 10 | ... | 20 | → |

BADGES   html

Default ❶   Success ❷   Warning ❹

PROGRESS BAR   html

FEEDBACK MESSAGES   html

Oh snap! Change a few things up and tr

Well done! You successfully read this ir

Heads up! This alert needs your attentic

TABLE SORTER

Last Name ▲	Language
Dent	Code
Dawson	English
Sixpack	English
Laukka	Finnish

REQUIRED FORM FIELDS

Name *

First   Last

CONTENT GROUPS

DYNAMIC INPUT HINTS   m

Leave a blank line for every new direction

Layout is the strategic arrangement of the elements in a visual design. It is the harmonious placement of type, image, line, shape, tone, colour, imagery and space. Layout can be applied to books and magazines, web pages and electronic documents, as well as interfaces, environments and controls.

The purpose of layout is to: create attractive visual relationships between elements; to organize (group/separate) visual information to make it easier to understand; to create emphasis, so the most important information is not overlooked; and to create direction, so that information is encountered in the correct order.

Print vs electronic media

Compared to layout for electronic media, layout for the printed page is comparatively straightforward. Although it requires a great deal of visual awareness, it is a singular task, as the dimensions, orientation and proportions of the page are fixed. Layout for electronic devices is a more multi-faceted challenge, as the same material may have to be repurposed for displays of different dimensions or orientations, or respond to changes in the user's context. The layout may have to flip, rotate, scale, minimize, resize or change order completely, depending on the capabilities of the display equipment and the current needs of the user and their surroundings.

Brand awareness may also be a factor in designing a layout. Decisions about colour, type and space may be influenced by corporate guidelines that stipulate how logos may be combined with other visual elements.

Layout for electronic media

Electronic media can be thought of as an infinite canvas of information, with the user display acting as a tiny 'window' through which fragments of this content may be viewed. Users may have to be reminded of off-screen notifications that can be pulled into view as required. Some visual information may be context specific, so it may be fully or partially hidden at times.

Evaluating layout

User research is an important tool in evaluating a layout. For example, observing or interviewing the user may reveal cultural factors that influence how they interpret or prioritize visual information. On a more qualitative level, eye- or gaze-tracking technologies allow us to measure how users navigate their way through visual information, so that we assess with some confidence whether or not they are providing the best visual experience.

5.12

5.12
Freedom Studios
The website for Freedom Studios, a contemporary theatre company, has the hallmarks of classical design: a consistent underlying grid; strong alignment of text and image; and a bold logo in the upper left-hand corner to act as an entry point.

Grids

Layout should be unified and consistent. Separate pages or screens have a shared framework so that users will recognize they belong together in spite of their differences.

Grids are a common way of creating this unity of visual design. A grid is a lattice of horizontal and vertical guides that are distributed across the page or screen. During the visual design stage, the grid provides a series of intersecting 'anchor-points' onto which the visual elements can be placed. The guides are only visible to the designer, who will remove or hide them once the layout is satisfactory. Grids are usually constructed around established divisions and proportions. A flexible grid is one which allows for variety in the arrangement of elements in different ways whilst preserving a recognizably consistent underlying structure.

5.13–5.16
Designing for various devices
Digital layout is not a simple matter of organizing elements on a screen of fixed dimensions, as if designing for a printed magazine spread (5.13). The components of a corresponding digital design may scale (5.14), reside off-screen on a navigable infinite canvas, with the device acting as a window (5.15), or rearrange completely to suit the device or platform (5.16). To design for a variety of devices and scenarios, the crucial thing is that the layout must have a strong visual hierarchy, including points of emphasis that direct the user and lead the eye.

Responsive design

For some years, designers have struggled with the Web as a replacement for print media because, unlike printed pages, web pages can be changed to any shape or size. Designers responded by creating pages that were required to be viewed at a particular size or by creating fluid layouts where the content would scale and move around depending on the size of the viewing frame. A huge amount of angst was suffered in the design community because the visual structure and typography of their work could be badly distorted by the medium of delivery.

More recently, the wide adoption of many more types of devices including smartphones and tablet computers has created a need for responsive design. Devices with varying capabilities for interaction and wildly differing screen sizes provide a real challenge for designers. Fortunately, it is now possible for a system to query a device's capabilities before sending any media to it. This means that, with some intelligent coding, a visual design can be dynamically adjusted to provide appropriate content for a particular device or platform. It also means that designers can create designs that are relevant to the device and the context in which it is being used.

5.13

5.14

5.15

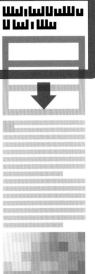

5.16

Typography is the art of selecting, combining and arranging different typefaces in order to create structure and meaning. When typography is used well, the appearance and placement of words can communicate just as much as the words themselves.

Typography can be used to create visual repetition, in order to create a relationship between sections of type that may be spatially disconnected. As well as possessing a distinctive personality, type can be adjusted to create contrasts in scale, colour and direction. White space around characters, words, and lines of text can also be adjusted to affect how the text will be perceived. In this way typography can create a visual hierarchy and organization. Sensitive choices about type can lead the eye around a page or screen, thus giving emphasis to particular pieces of text and encouraging users to interact with specific elements.

Type can be a very powerful visual instrument for creating emotional responses. Users can often identify very strongly with different categories of type. Some digital typefaces can have the appearance of erratic hand-drawn lettering, creating a sense of freedom and individuality that may resonate very strongly with the reader. Conversely, elegant and geometric typefaces may provide a reassuring sense of orderliness, reliability and of efficiency. Users of business or legal services will have their expectations reassured by an appropriately business-like typeface.

Digital type

Many familiar typefaces come pre-installed on computers or bundled with software, but newer and more specialized typefaces need to be purchased and correctly installed. In order for special typefaces to render correctly on a device, the chosen typeface must be installed on it or otherwise embedded into the document or application being viewed. Designs may not appear as the designer intended if the user does not have the typeface installed. This is just one example of why interactive designs should always be tested on typical user set-ups rather than on the development system used by the designer.

5.17
Typography as part of the experience
Design agency Analogue designed a bespoke logo for the menus of The Hummingbird Kitchen and Bar, but the type was also forged into a striking exterior display. Typography is not just a matter of selecting an installed font from a drop-down list: it can be a tangible and defining part of an experience.

5.17

Images, especially photographic images, can add tremendous value to an experience. Images can act as visual aids to assist memory and understanding. Images can shape user expectations by giving them visual models of what lies ahead. Images can illustrate the preferred mode of interaction, so that the experience is more intuitive and less frustrating.

Images can exist as digital files to be located and retrieved for display on devices of various dimensions, or they may be printed on packaging or surfaces of fixed dimensions. Different types of image display require different methods to be applied when they are devised and created. Displaying images, particularly moving images, can require considerable resources to be available for transmission and display. For this reason image files are usually compressed by removing information that is not normally noticed by the viewer in a way that does not degrade the experience of viewing the image. Planning an enjoyable, image-rich experience requires an understanding of these technical requirements and many others. In addition, there are number of factors to consider at various stages of designing an interactive experience that uses static or moving images:

→ Which devices or surfaces will the image be displayed upon? What are their capabilities for handling and displaying images?

→ How can the image respond to different devices and platforms?

→ How is the quality of the image related to the quality of the user experience?

→ Is image metadata required to utilize the image?

→ What is the communication function of the image?

→ Will there be any environmental conditions that affect the fidelity or meaning of the image?

→ What emotional impact, positive or negative, will the image have on the user?

5.18

http://codebarre.tv

5.18
Bar Code/Code Barre
'Bar Code/Code Barre'
is a collection of short
documentaries inviting you
to 'pick an item and listen to
its story'. In this film about
technological gadgets by Florian
Geyer, a young lady converses
with her friend in sign language
via smart-phone. Although
modern technology is capable
of creating eye-boggling
visuals for screen or print, the
film illustrates that sometimes
relatively simple, low-resolution
images are all that two friends
need to share a positive and
intimate experience.

Copyright

Copyright is a set of principles, backed up by various international laws, whereby the creator of an artistic work can authorize or restrict the re-use of their work. Copyright applies to images, written works such as poetry and lyrics, typefaces, and even some types of performance. As designers, we have a legal obligation to respect creator rights, and we should only make use of images where permission has been explicitly granted for the image to be used.

Permission is usually obtained in exchange for a fee, and sometimes the rights to re-use an image may be negotiated directly with the creator. Often, however, the image rights are handled by large agencies that have vast, searchable databases of easily licensed photographs and illustrations.

In a project which involves the use of many images, a picture researcher may be employed to investigate who the copyright holders are, and negotiate the scope and terms of the image re-use. Securing expensive copyright licences may be beyond the scope of a small-budget project, but there are some lower cost alternatives.

Creative Commons is a licensing system whereby the permission to re-use or adapt a creative work is clearly expressed. Creators can assign a Creative Commons licence to each work, permitting re-use, modification, or commercial exploitation of their work. Image search engines like Google Images and Flickr allow you to filter search results so that only unrestricted or Creative Commons images are displayed in search results. You will still need to check the wording of the licence, but it is less likely that you will have to negotiate with creators or agents.

Ethics

Images can be a very seductive element in any experience: interactive applications, print, and environmental. This is not to say that an experience always lives up to the promise of the image used to represent it. In recent years, publishers, advertisers and consumers have been more alert to the ways in which images can deceive. For example, airbrushing and manipulation of images in software such as Photoshop can create unrealistic ideals of beauty or health. In addition, unimaginative or ill-informed choices of images can reinforce harmful attitudes, such as the prejudice caused by misrepresenting different cultural and ethnic groups.

Unrealistic imagery can create unrealistic expectations, which will inevitably lead to disappointment. This can have a negative impact on individual self-esteem, and even on society in general. Images should be used in a way that promotes a realistic portrayal of the world and our place in it.

5.19
Conveying the message
For their portfolio brochure, Analogue carefully constructed a cardboard Apple Mac, complete with shards of explosive colour. A computer-generated illustration could have denoted the same thing, but the photographs of the painstakingly crafted paper models convey much more about the agency's attention to detail, as well as their irreverent and playful attitude to their design heritage.

To prepare for this activity you need to complete the Exploring Solutions activity (Chapter 4, page 132) and read about prototyping tools earlier in this chapter. In this activity the aim is to produce a 'rapid prototype' quickly and easily that simulates the interactive design so that users can use it and give feedback. Because it is a prototype, there is no need to devote time or effort to make the back-end technology work. Where dynamic data is required, such as search results, this can be replaced by static data. If you find that something is difficult to simulate in the prototype then it can be left out and its function explained to the user at the point where they encounter it.

If you are sceptical about the benefits of prototyping then we urge you to give it a try. It is a step toward participatory design and for some designers it may seem like relinquishing control. In reality, it will validate the hard work done in researching and specifying the design and save huge amounts of wasted time and money on designs that simply do not work as well as they should.

5.20

Design and amending the activity

We have designed this activity so that it can be done using little more than pencil, paper and Scotch Magic Tape. The interface and elements at every stage are sketched on individual pieces of paper or thin card. It may save time to create the elements in software and print them out depending on the complexity of the interactions.

The prototype is made interactive by an assistant who moves the interface elements in and out of the 'interface' in response to the actions that the user takes. This is a low-tech approach, but has the advantage of being really easy to set up, incredibly flexible and less intimidating for some users. We also think that users are more open with their comments because they can see that the prototype is clearly a work in progress. It is easy to make notes on the interface during a usability test and to change the flow of interaction if required.

Digital prototype of activity

If you would prefer to create a digital prototype then there are many online tools that do the job. Some simulate the paper prototyping method by simply presenting the interface on a computer screen, with the option to retain a hand-drawn style (pencil.evolus.vn). They usually include a library of common interface graphics. More sophisticated prototyping tools include libraries of high-fidelity interface graphics that appear real to the user and offer functions to simulate links and transitions. At the time of writing, new web apps such as Fluidui (fluidui.com) are beginning to appear. These have the additional benefit of being able to run prototype simulations on real devices and for prototypes to be stored in the cloud for remote testing and feedback.

5.20
Paper prototyping
Paper prototypes are the ultimate low-fidelity approach to making an interface real and allow simple testing of your designs. Detailed paper prototyping techniques are discussed by the author of *Paper Prototyping*, Carolyn Snyder, at her website: paperprototyping.com.

Activity 5
Build a prototype

Step 1 – Preparing to build

Review your notes and sketches defining the solution that you created in Activity 4. Make a list of each of the interface elements that are needed to build the solution.

Step 2 – Make the interface and interface elements

Cut thin card sheets to a similar shape of a typical display on a target device. These do not need to be the same size as the device display and it may help to make them slightly larger to make the process less fiddly. Draw all the interface elements needed on paper (using the list created in Step 1) and cut them out with scissors. If colour is required then this can be applied using crayon shading or by using coloured paper.

Step 3 – Build

Starting with the user's entry point to the interactive application, position the interface elements and stick them down with the tape. Consider all user choices available at the entry point and create cards designed to replace the current card for each of the choices that can be made. Alternatively, work at the element level and create a stack of different elements that the assistant can apply to the current card to update it in response to the user's choice. Continue in this way to build the prototype until it is complete.

Step 4 – Try it out

Revisit the user goals that were defined in Activity 4 and work through the prototype to review how the user will achieve each goal, and make any adjustments that are necessary for the prototype to work as expected. You will use the prototype to validate the design. For example, the first goal states: 'To be aware of all relevant opportunities as they arise.' A solution for this goal could be to design a status indicator that appears at some stage in the user's interaction. If it has, and the user acknowledges that they have achieved that goal, then no problem! If they continue without understanding the significance of the status indicator then the solution has not been validated. You may find it useful to write a statement of what constitutes success for each goal and refer to it during user testing.

Step 5 – Test it

Now you have confidence in the design it is important to test it with potential users. Depending on the size and the scope of the project, you will need to organize a session with people in the target groups to explore the prototype and validate the design. It is a good idea to record the session because what users say can contain a rich source of clues as to how they are responding to the design.

Outcomes

If this activity has been successful then many of the benefits of producing a prototype will have become clear. Potential problems in the design of the original solution are revealed and opportunities for simplifying and enhancing the user experience become more obvious; both major benefits of what should be a quick and very low cost technique.

Some would argue that testing an interface design away from the computer allows better communication between the designer and the user. Others may say that it is impossible to simulate sophisticated computer interactions like swiping and contextual menus with paper. This activity has hopefully provided an opportunity for you to try an open and enquiring approach to the important initial stages of a project's development.

We hope this book has given you an overview of design for the user experience: the factors of human behaviour and environment that shape our responses to experiences; the designed and constructed elements that contribute to positive experiences; and the tools and methods that designers can incorporate into a working process in order to deliver and assess positive experiences.

Design is for you

This book argues that design is for other people; not for us. Being a more empathetic designer requires that you step out of yourself, and recognize that different people have different needs and expectations. We hope this book will encourage you to be innovative in your design responses, and above all to acquire and retain empathy with the end user throughout the design process.

User experience design is not a simple matter of conforming to international standards or established design processes. It is about respect for the user. Products and services do not have value in themselves. Experiences are more important than the products or services themselves, and this has to be considered if we are going to add value to the world with our creative efforts.

'We hope this book will encourage you to be innovative in your design responses, and above all to acquire and retain empathy with the end user throughout the design process.'

Promotion of a UXD approach

Design for user experience can be driven by thinking about how other people feel, and by reading the existing studies on user behaviour. The real test of our commitment to UXD will be a willingness to ask real users what they think. By real users, we mean strangers, not friends or classmates or our family. The people close to us are predisposed to say what we want to hear. They will not successfully represent the target demographic.

A real user has a vested interest in improving the experience of work or play that we are designing for them. The motive of a real user will be to increase their own satisfaction. To this end, they are more likely to tell us things that we need to hear, even if the outcome is more work and different ideas.

For a designer, one of the most intimidating things about UXD methods is that we are actively inviting other people to be critical of our work and of our ideas. What is more, we may have to leave the comfort of our familiar environment to hear this and respond constructively at all times.

A willingness to take these steps requires the development of character. A thick skin will help and other personal attributes will grow with experience. We will learn courage, resilience, curiosity, humility and critical thinking. These changes in our values as designers will set us apart as the architects of excellent experiences.

Books

Ambrose, G. and Harris, P. (2011)
Basics Design 02: Layout.
AVA Publishing
A visually inspiring book which explains the key principles of layout for the page and, in the new editing, relates these fundamentals to layout for the screen.

Antoniou, G. and Harmelen, F. van (2004)
A Semantic Web Primer. **MIT**
One of the most important things about semantics is that the organizational structure that is used must be consistent and have the potential to evolve as new information is incorporated. *A Semantic Web Primer* thoroughly explains the requirements of such a structure, going into detail about the alternative methods for managing metadata: the hidden 'labels' that define how information is categorized and inter-related.

Barnum, C.M. (2010)
Usability Testing Essentials.
Morgan Kaufmann
A readable and pragmatic book about the questions you must ask before researching users and usability, as well as the methods for conducting the research.

Beck, R.C. (2003)
Motivation: Theories and principles.
Prentice Hall
A comprehensive reference about human motivation, derived from experiments and observations of human (and animal) behaviour. This book will give an insight into the biological forces that are at the root of our choices and preferences.

Blythe, M.A. (2003)
Funology: From usability to enjoyment.
Kluwer Academic
A collection of research papers into the relationship between interactions and pleasure. After a useful discussion of the nature of fun, it moves on to more specific case studies of enjoyable interactions between people and technology.

Brown, D.M. (2011)
Communicating Design: Developing website documentation for design and planning.
New Riders
A helpful guidebook on professional documentation and presentation. It shows how to organize and format the findings from user research, and the plans for the design and implementation of a product or service.

BS EN ISO 9241-210:2010
Ergonomics of human–system interaction. Human-centred design for interactive systems.
ISO/BSI
At the time of writing, this is the international standard most relevant to UXD. It is called Part 210 because it forms just one part of a group of standards within the Ergonomics of Human–System Interaction. Other areas include Part 11: Guidance on usability and Part 920: Guidance on tactile and haptic interactions.

Buxton, B. (2007)
Sketching User Experience.
Morgan Kaufmann
Sketching can mean drawing, improvizing, prototyping and iterating. Through a series of personal anecdotes and thoughtful case studies, Bill Buxton shows how investigating the user context is a crucial part of the design problem.

Cooper, A., Reimann, R. and Cronin, D. (2007)
About Face 3: The essentials of interaction design. **Wiley**
A highly recommended read: it explains and promotes a holistic approach to interaction design, and provides detailed, useful guidance on all stages of a UXD process.

Csikszentmihalyi, M. (2000)
Beyond Boredom and Anxiety: Experiencing flow in work and play.
Jossey-Bass
Mihaly Csikszentmihalyi (pronounced 'cheek-sent-me-high-yee') has spent decades investigating happiness and motivation. His studies are based upon interviews with experts, such as mountaineers and concert pianists, who regularly achieve a state of 'flow', in which an activity becomes so engrossing and intrinsically motivated. Here, Csikszentmihalyi explains what is required to help create and maintain a flow state.

Garrett, J.J. (2011)
The Elements of User Experience: User-centered design for the Web and beyond.
New Riders
The elements of user experience deconstructs the experience of using a website into a tier of interactions, from the initial visual appearance of the page down to the underlying business objectives of the website owner. The book provides a clear and universal framework for discussing the user experience with partners in the design process.

Hall, S. (2007)
This Means This, This Means That: A user's guide to semiotics.
Laurence King
In a series of intriguing and vividly illustrated questions, this book introduces many of the key ideas of Semiotics, as well as the histories of the thinkers behind them. It shows the various ways in which we find (or overlook) the meaning in visual messages.

Koster, R. (2005)
A Theory of Fun for Game Design.
AZ: Paraglyph
A conversational philosophy on why games are fun, and how this can be applied to other interactions.

Krug, S. (2006)
Don't Make Me Think!: a Common Sense Approach to Web Usability.
New Riders Publishing
An often-cited and immensely readable guide to designing usable web-pages, with lots of clear examples of and subtle design changes can eliminate user anxiety.

Kuniavsky, M. (2003)
Observing the User Experience: A practitioner's guide to user research.
Morgan Kaufmann
A detailed and reassuring guide to planning, conducting and utilizing user research. The book explains how to select the most appropriate research method, and how to undertake and document the different types of observations and interviews.

Lidwell, W., Holden, K. and Butler, J. (2010)
Universal Principles of Design: 125 ways to enhance usability, influence perception, increase appeal, make better design decisions, and teach through design.
Rockport
A principle is something that has been proven, over time, to work. In design studies, some of these principles may be based on science and mathematics; or the ergonomics of how the human body has evolved over millennia. Other established principles arise from our shared exposure to works of art across the centuries. Universal principles of design gather together some of the most fundamental and immutable 'rules of thumb' when designing for human beings, and show how they still apply to emerging platforms and technologies.

Lupton, E. (2010)
Thinking with Type: A critical guide for designers, writers, editors and students.
Princeton Architectural
A detailed overview of the history, philosophy, art and science of typography for different media.

Maslow, A.H. and Frager, R. (1987)
Motivation and Personality.
Addison Wesley
Maslow was an American psychologist who devised the famous 'hierarchy of needs'. This is the book in which his model is explained. Usually depicted as a triangle, the model suggests that certain 'lower' physiological needs (such as security and hunger) must be satisfied before 'higher' needs (such as belonging and esteem) can be addressed.

McKee, R. (1999)
Story: Substance, structure, style, and the principles of screenwriting.
Methuen
McKee explains how narrative structure can be simplified to a few crucial features, but still provide endless variation. The principles of character, goals and antagonism that McKee discusses in relation to movies can be related to all other types of human experience.

Mulder, S. and Yaar, Z. (2007)
The User is Always Right: A practical guide to creating and using personas for the Web.
New Riders
An enthusiastic manifesto and practical guide to personas explaining what they are, why to use them and how to create them.

Nemeth, C. (2004)
Human Factors Methods for Design: Making systems human-centered.
CRC Press
A technical guide to designing processes that are sympathetic to the limits of human attention, memory and understanding.

Norman, D.A. (2005)
Emotional Design: Why we love (or hate) everyday things.
Basic Books
Don Norman is a prominent champion of user-centred design. This book is a persuasive and entertaining reminder that efficiency and usability are not the only objectives of a user-centred approach; human emotions and aesthetics are also an important part of a positive user experience.

Olins, W. (2008)
Wally Olins: The brand handbook.
Thames & Hudson
A visually rich book about why brands matter to businesses and users, and the effort required to create and nurture them.

Porter, J. (2008)
Designing for the Social Web.
Pearson Education
This book shows, with many entertaining and clear examples, how social enterprise succeeds when the people behind it are sensitive to the social needs of the users.

Salen, K. and Zimmerman, E. (2004)
Rules of Play: Game design fundamentals.
MIT
A very thorough and entertaining text book about the mechanics, rules and challenges of playing games, and how the intelligent design of games corresponds to aspects of human behaviour.

Snyder, Carolyn (2003)
Paper Prototyping: The fast and easy way to design and refine user interfaces.
Morgan Kaufmann
This book explains every last detail of paper prototyping techniques, including what type of sticky tape to use and how to test prototypes with users.

Tufte, E.R. (2001)
The Visual Display of Quantitative Information
Graphics Press
A critical overview of the history of information graphics, it explores the ambiguities and the ethics of translating data into clear and accurate visuals.

Weinman, L. and Karp, A. (2003)
Designing Web graphics 4.
New Riders
This book provides many of the answers about how digital images should be planned, formatted and optimized for different platforms. It is an active dialogue that will guide the designer in their design iterations.

Websites

Don Norman Blog Don Norman is credited with inventing the term 'user experience'. His blog includes articles about designing for people, and information about his books and appearances at international events.
www.jnd.org

Pleasure and Pain
Whitney Hess is a UX consultant and empathy evangelist. She blogs about UX tools and methods, and about decency and respect in design.
whitneyhess.com/blog

Smashing Magazine
A web magazine about all aspects of UXD, from user research and client liaison, to coding and development for specific platforms.
uxdesign.smashingmagazine.com

Stack Exchange: User Experience
The world is full of people who have learned the hard way, so that you do not need to! Stack Exchange is a forum where experienced designers will respond to questions about user experience design.
ux.stackexchange.com

The Fun Theory
The fun theory is a project which seeks to encourage responsible behaviour by injecting more fun into everyday activities. Examples include the transformation of a bottle-bank into a quick-response target game to entice people into recycling more bottles.
www.thefuntheory.com

The UX Booth
A blog of articles about user experience, usability, research, design tools, and working with clients.
www.uxbooth.com

W3CStandards
The World Wide Web Consortium (W3C) is an organization that works to define international standards for web development. It is the W3C that arbitrates what is 'valid' in terms of web applications and communications. Its standards page has the latest information about proposed standards for the emerging platforms and technologies.
www.w3.org/standards

WAI
The Web Accessibility Initiative resource 'Involving Users in Web Accessibility Evaluation' at www.w3.org/WAI/eval/users provides guidance on including people with disabilities in design projects.

A–B Testing
This testing method compares two variants of the same website or app. The 'B' version of the website would typically have only one distinct difference to the interface of the 'A' version, such as a 'call-to-action' that is a different colour, shape or position. By comparing the conversion data from the two sites, designers can see which of the two was most effective, and iterate accordingly.

Aesthetics
Those features that we perceive as being beautiful, or not. Aesthetics are often considered as important as other factors in the user's experience.

Agile Development
An iterative approach to developing software that strives to make prompt, incremental improvements to software based upon changing circumstances and evolving design requirements.

Analytics
Monitoring the traffic to websites generates tremendous amounts of complex data. Analytics are a tool for harvesting data and presenting it in various ways as readable graphs.

Antagonism
A force of opposition in a story or game, typically a 'bad guy', a time constraint, or a force of nature.

Augmented Reality (AR)
A technology that can detect images via the camera in digital devices, and then superimpose context-specific media onto the image.

Back-end
The hidden 'machinery' of a system that the user does not directly encounter, but which is still required for the experience to function. See also 'Front-end'.

Behavioural
A type of emotional human response. In UXD, behavioural responses are the ones that we feel when occupied with using a product or service.

Brainstorming
An approach to problem solving and idea generation. The strategy is to rapidly generate as many solutions as possible without judgement, and then, only once this ideas phase is over, move on to evaluate them more soberly.

Card-sorting
A research method in which a user is given a stack of cards with key terms written on them. The user is asked to sort the cards into logical groups, creating an organizational structure that makes sense to them. The test is repeated with multiple users to reveal patterns of consistent behaviour and expectation.

Causality
The principle describing how actions are understood to have logical consequences.

Competitive Advantage
Both the features or benefits of a service or product that sets it apart from its competitors, as well as the corporate strategy of identifying and exploiting these features and benefits.

Context
The diverse set of circumstances that surround and impact upon an experience.

Conversion
An action by a user that represents some kind of commitment to a product or service. A visitor to a website is 'converted' if they respond to a 'call to action', which may be to subscribe to a service or choose a product.

Copyright
A collection of protective laws that grant a creator some control over how a literary or artistic work may be used. Computer code is protected as a 'literary' work. Copyright can be traded.

Creative Commons
A licensing system for digital media. A creator can attach a Creative Commons license to a digital work (such as a photograph or a music track) to make clear whether or not the work may be freely used elsewhere.

CSS – Cascading Style Sheets
Whereas HTML is the mark-up language that defines the content and structure of a webpage, CSS is the coding language used to describe the visual elements, including position, scale and colour.

Demographic
A group of people with a common characteristic, such as age or gender; often used to describe a target group of users.

Empathy
The human capacity to understand how other people feel.

Ergonomics
A discipline of design and engineering that studies the relationship between people and their surroundings.

Ethnography
A type of observational research that observes subjects in their normal environment.

Extrinsic
External to, or beyond itself. 'Extrinsic' is a term that can be applied to human motivation, meaning that the user undertakes a task in response to external pressures or influences.

Eye-tracking
See Gaze-tracking

Flow
According to psychologist Mihaly Csikszentmihalyi, flow is the mental state of somebody who is fully immersed in a focused activity.

Focus Group
A selection of target users who are assembled by a researcher or designer in order to share their ideas and opinions about design problems and solutions.

Front-end
The 'front-end' of a product or service is the 'surface': the aesthetics; the typography, imagery and interaction design that provide the user with direct sensory cues. See also 'Back-end'.

Gantt Chart
A project management tool devised by engineer Henry Gannt: a timeline which shows the sequence and interdependencies of all the discrete tasks within a larger project.

Gaze-tracking
Gaze-tracking (or eye-tracking) is a technology that records the precise direction of your gaze. In user-testing, gaze-tracking can identify the areas of a visual display that capture the user's attention.

Gestalt
Gestalt is a field of human psychology that attempts to explain how we make sense of visual information.

Goal
A specific objective to be accomplished, a goal may help define the requirements of an experience, or provide a benchmark for user testing.

Haptic
Anything related to the sense of touch. Haptic technologies are those that are designed to provide some kind of touch-based interface or feedback.

Hierarchy
A hierarchy is an organizing structure in which people, information or objects are arranged by rank or importance: the most significant appear at the top, and the least are found at the bottom.

HTML – Hypertext Markup Language
HTML is the mark-up language that describes how the content of a webpage should be organized and hyperlinked.

Icon
In the field of semiotics, an icon is a particular type of sign that has some kind of resemblance to the thing it signifies.

Index
In the field of semiotics, an index is a particular type of sign that points to, or indicates, something else that has meaning or purpose, such as a depression in a surface indicating a good place to put your thumb.

Information Architecture
The principle of specifying how a mass of information should be logically arranged, navigated and extended.

Intellectual Property
Any creative work protected by copyright. Because creators can sell licenses allowing their copyrighted work to be reused, Intellectual Property is a valuable commodity that is carefully managed and protected.

Intrinsic
Belonging to, or contained within, itself. 'Intrinsic' is a term that can be applied to human motivation, meaning that the user undertakes a task with no external pressure or influence.

Intuitive
Intuition is the sensation of immediate understanding that does not require any form of instruction, interpretation or prior experience. In truth, there is no such thing as an intuitive experience, as all new encounters will rely on existing knowledge and experience.

ISO – International Organization for Standardization
An international body that defines global standards of safety and quality.

Iteration
A process of repetition. In UXD, the aim of repeating the process is to continuously and successively improve upon the previous version of the design.

Metadata
Data about data. It often accompanies digital media in order to provide extra information, such as technical data or content description.

Metaphor
Something familiar referred to in a different context to help make sense of something unfamiliar.

Mnemonics
A kind of encoding pattern or system or recognition used to make more complex information more memorable. 'One collar, two sleeves' is a mnemonic to recall the correct number of specific consonants in the word 'necessary'.

Persona
A persona is a fictitious character created when considering the suitability of a design solution for an archetypal user. Personas are based upon research into real people, rather than an imagined 'ideal' user.

PET Design – Persuasion, Emotion, Trust
A methodology for UX research and design centred on the psychology of human behaviour, pioneered by Human Factors Inc.

Platform
An underlying system or infrastructure, such as an operating system (Windows, Android or Symbian). Because ubiquitous web-based tools (Facebook, Twitter) are not loyal to specific hardware technologies or operating systems, these can also be regarded as independent platforms.

Protagonist
The 'hero/heroine' of a narrative.

Prototype
A mock-up or early build of a product or service, developed quickly to illustrate a design concept, or so that it can be used in testing in order to define exactly what type of refinements are required.

Qualitative
Statistical data concerned with the immeasurable, such as the opinions of users.

Quantitative
Statistical data that is measurable and comparable, such as the numbers of visitors to a website.

Rapid Prototyping
A method of using very simple materials, or specialist design templates, in order to quickly produce a working prototype so that a design concept can be tested.

Reflective
A type of emotional human response. In UXD, behavioural responses are the ones that we feel when occupied with using a product or service.

Responsive Design
An approach to digital design that enables information to be supplied to a target device in a format that adapts to its display characteristics.

Scenario
A story (or scene) that describes a set of circumstances (see also persona and context).

Schema
A model or structure of information that is created by, and for, the individual's mind. Schemata are our own personal information architectures.

Semantics
The science and study of 'meaning'. In UXD, it describes a conscious effort to organize information in a way that users will find meaningful.

SEO – Search Engine Optimization
A strategic attempt to make webpages highly visible to relevant searches made with search engines such as Google. A number of techniques are used, including embedding key-words into the HTML of the page, as well as maximizing the number of other links to the website from elsewhere.

Stakeholders
A person or organization with an interest in a project or who may be affected by the existence of a project.

Symbol
In the field of semiotics, a symbol is a particular type of sign that has a completely arbitrary and negotiated relationship with thing it signifies, such as a red-light signifying 'stop'.

Task Modelling
A UXD methodology that attempts to recognize the way that people approach a real-world objective (or task), and designing experiences to accommodate this task-oriented approach.

Tree Testing
This is a technique used to test a proposed information architecture. The test participant is given a search term, and then descends the hierarchy of the information architecture, selecting from the available categories (or 'branches') at each level, in pursuit of the search term. If the structure is appropriate, the user should arrive at the target item with few detours.

UCD – User Centred Design
An iterative approach to design that involves the end user at various stages of the design process in order to create a system that is sensitive to their environment and the tasks they need to accomplish.

UI – User Interface
The designed space in which an interaction occurs between a user and a system or product.

Usability
The extent to which a designed experience is found to be usable by its intended users.

Usability Testing
The process of testing and assessing a product or service in order to discover how usable it is for the intended users.

UX – User Experience

How a designed system affects the user and elicits feelings and attitudes that remain associated with that system.

Validation
The process of checking that something meets predetermined criteria or a set of rules.

Values
Standards that determine what we believe to be important or correct and influence how we act.

Visceral
A type of emotional human response. In UXD, visceral responses are the 'gut' feelings that we have before we consider the experience on an intellectual level.

W3C – World Wide Web Consortium
An international community that develops open standards to ensure the long-term growth of the Web.

Wireframes
A scheme for depicting the planned arrangement of key elements in an interface design. The plan will omit fine details and specific content, replacing these with a lattice of empty rectangular placeholders, in order to show only the underlying visual hierarchy of the interface.

Cover image: Cavey images courtesy of Analogue Creative Ltd. madebyanalogue.co.uk

Page 2: Site specific projection courtesy of UrbanScreen. urbanscreen.com

Page 11: AIGA Design Archives courtesy of Second Story (part of SapientNitro). secondstory.com

Chapter 1

Page 15: Style-Passport images courtesy of Maek Design. maekdesign.com

Page 16: Coastal Path image courtesy of Carol Smith. carolsmithphotography.com

Pages 18–19: Out My Window (2010), National Film Board of Canada. interactive. nfb.ca/#/outmywindow

Page 21: Images of Michael J Godfrey, Jennifer Dolan and Norman Lau courtesy of Second Story (part of SapientNitro). secondstory.com

Pages 24–25: Wondermind images courtesy of Preloaded Ltd/Tate. preloaded.com

Pages 26–27: Jeego images courtesy of Maek Design. maekdesign.com

Page 29: The Car People image courtesy of Code Computerlove Ltd. codecomputerlove. com

Page 31: Collaborative methods image courtesy of Code Computerlove Ltd. codecomputerlove.com

Pages 32–33: Identification of deliverables image courtesy of Code Computerlove Ltd. codecomputerlove. com

Pages 44–45: Dulwich Picture Gallery images courtesy of Reading Room Ltd. readingroom. com

Chapter 2

Page 47: Sqoshi images courtesy of Keep it Usable. keepitusable.com

Page 48: Images of Lisa Duddington and Ricardo Ortega courtesy of Keep it Usable. keepitusable.com

Page 51: The User Experience Machine image courtesy of Keep it Usable. keepitusable.com

Pages 52–53: Projection images courtesy of UrbanScreen. urbanscreen.com.

Page 55: Spotify Box prototypes images courtesy of Jordi Parra, Umea Institute of Design 2011. blog.zenona.com

Page 57: Axon images courtesy of Preloaded. preloaded.com

Page 59: Plan B images courtesy of Rona Marin-Miller (Interaction Designer) and Kerr Marin-Miller (Developer). ronamarinmiller.com and kerrmarin.com.

Page 61: Allan Gravgaard Madsen record sleeve courtesy of Michael Hansen. michaelhansenwork.dk

Page 63: Cavey images courtesy of Analogue Creative Ltd. madebyanalogue.co.uk

Pages 66–67: Flowella images courtesy of Megan Payne.

Chapter 3

Page 71: Lisn Music™ images courtesy of Analogue Creative Ltd. madebyanalogue. co.uk

Page 73: Adidas Predator® X images courtesy of Dinosaur (UK) Ltd. dinosaur.co.uk

Pages 74–75: National Museums of Scotland mask app images courtesy of Preloaded Ltd/ National Museums of Scotland. preloaded. com

Page 76: Image courtesy of Chris Atherton.

Page 79: British Thyroid Foundation Children's animation image courtesy of British Thyroid Foundation and Numiko Ltd. numiko.com

Page 81: The Co-operative posters courtesy of Dinosaur (UK) Ltd. dinosaur.co.uk

Pages 82–83: Tides and Times images courtesy of Maek Design. maekdesign.com.

Page 83 (bottom image): Tides and Times kiosk image courtesy of Peter Trimming. petertrimming.webs.com

Page 85: A&R Photographic images courtesy of Maek Design. maekdesign.com

Page 87: Launchball images courtesy of Preloaded. preloaded.com

Page 93: Portobello Star website images courtesy of Analogue Creative Ltd. madebyanalogue.co.uk

Page 101: Linkem image courtesy of Preloaded Ltd/ Somethin' Else/ Channel 4 Education. preloaded.com

Page 103: Bla Bla (2011) courtesy of The National Film Board of Canada. blabla. nfb.ca/#/blabla

Page 105 (top image) © 2010 iamgavin. com, all rights reserved. Bottom images © 2010 Hufton & Crowe. huftonandcrow.com. Images courtesy of Aecom (Strategy Plus). aecom.com

Chapter 4

Page 109: Supersight images courtesy of Preloaded Ltd/ Somethin' Else/ Channel 4 Education. preloaded.com

Pages 112–113: Make Bradford British images courtesy of Numiko. numiko.com

Page 115: Terence Higgins Trust website image courtesy of Reading Room Ltd. readingroom.com

Pages 116–117: Personas courtesy of Rebecca Topps. toppsusability.co.uk

Pages 122–123: Merlin image courtesy of David Bellona. davidbellona.com

Chapter 5

Page 131: Permission to reproduce extracts from ISO 9241-210:2010. Ergonomics of human-system interaction -- Part 210: Human-centred design for interactive systems is granted by BSI. British Standards can be obtained in PDF or hard copy formats from the BSI online shop: bsigroup. com/Shop or by contacting BSI Customer Services for hard copies only: Tel: +44 (0)20 8996 9001. Email: cservices@bsigroup.com.

Page 139: Augmented reality images courtesy of Kei Shiratori / Takeshi Mukai / Younghyo Bak (Matilde Inc.) arart.info

Page 141: All Star Lanes images courtesy of Maek Design. maekdesign.com

Page 143: Timeless image courtesy of Justin Chen. justinchendesign.com

Page 147: UI stencil image courtesy of William Sjahrial. willsjah.com

Page 149: Hierarchy and navigation image courtesy of David Bellona. davidbellona.com

Pages 150–151: Cart sorting tool image courtesy of Optimal Workshop. optimalworkshop.com

Page 153: Presenting and amending prototypes images courtesy of Axure Software Solutions. axure.com

Page 155: Patternry Open image courtesy of Axure Software Solutions. axure.com

Page 157: Freedom Studios image courtesy of Analogue Creative Ltd. madebyanalogue. co.uk

Page 161: The Hummingbird Kitchen and Bar images courtesy of Analogue Creative Ltd. madebyanalogue.co.uk

Page 163: Code Barre images (2011) courtesy of National Film Board of Canada and ARTE France

Page 165: Portfolio brochure images courtesy of Analogue Creative Ltd. madebyanalogue. co.uk

Page 166: Paper prototyping image courtesy of David Bellona. davidbellona.com

All reasonable attempts have been made to trace, clear and credit the copyright holders of the images reproduced in this book. However, if any credits have been inadvertently omitted, the publisher will endeavour to incorporate amendments in future editions.

Gavin and Peter would like to thank
the following people for their help and
support in the writing and production
of this book:

Alison Allanwood

Alex Anderson

Chris Atherton

Michelle, Mabel and Jacob Beare

Julie Beeler

Garry Byrne

Lisa Duddington

David Eccles

Chris Gibbons

Mick Gornall

Juliet Ibbotson

Georgia Kennedy

Ricardo Ortega

Megan Payne

Jacqui Sayers

Martyn Shaw

Leonie Taylor

Rebecca Topps

The students and teaching team of the
Media Technology programmes at the
University of Central Lancashire, UK.